D1062065

HAS THE LORD INDEED SPOKEN ONLY THROUGH MOSES?

A Study of the Biblical Portrait of Miriam

SOCIETY
OF BIBLICAL
LITERATURE

DISSERTATION SERIES

J. J. M. Roberts, Old Testament Editor
Charles Talbert, New Testament Editor

Number 84

HAS THE LORD INDEED SPOKEN ONLY THROUGH MOSES?
A Study of the Biblical Portrait of Miriam

by
Rita J. Burns

Rita J. Burns

HAS THE LORD INDEED SPOKEN ONLY THROUGH MOSES?

A Study of the Biblical Portrait of Miriam

Scholars Press
Atlanta, Georgia

KRAUSS LIBRARY
LUTHERAN SCHOOL OF THEOLOGY AT CHICAGO
1100 EAST 55TH STREET
CHICAGO, ILLINOIS - 60615

HAS THE LORD INDEED SPOKEN
ONLY THROUGH MOSES?

A Study of the Biblical Portrait of Miriam

Rita J. Burns

BS
58Ø
, M 54
B 87
1987

Ph.D., 1980
Marquette University

Advisor:
John Sheehan, S.J.

© 1987
Society of Biblical Literature

Library of Congress Cataloging-in-Publication Data

Burns, Rita J., 1945–
 Has the Lord indeed spoken only through Moses?.

 (Dissertation series / Society of Biblical Literature
; no. 84)
 Originally presented as the author's thesis
(Ph.D.)–Marquette University, 1980.
 Bibliography: p.
 1. Miriam (Biblical figure) 2. Bible. O.T.–Biography
I. Title. II. Series: Dissertation series
(Society of Biblical Literature) ; no. 84.
BS580.M54B87 1986   222'.10924   86-6545
ISBN 0-89130-964-0
ISBN 0-89130-965-9 (pbk.)

Printed in the United States of America

KRAUSS LIBRARY
LUTHERAN SCHOOL OF THEOLOGY AT CHICAGO
1100 EAST 55th STREET
CHICAGO, ILLINOIS ▪ 60615

Contents

1

Introduction

In the sixth chapter of the prophet Micah the Lord summons Israel to court. There the God of Israel testifies to the divine ḥesed shown in the formative period of Israel's history. The deliverance from Egypt and the gift of the land are cited. Moreover, says the Divinity, "I sent before you Moses, Aaron, and Miriam."[1]

If one turns to the narrative accounts of this early period in Israel's story, one finds there a plethora of material about the leading figures, Moses and Aaron. But who is this Miriam whom the Lord also sent?

The often-forgotten figure whom the Lord also sent is mentioned in seven texts of the Bible and she has central stage in only two of these texts. She first appears in Exod 15:20-21 leading the women in dance and song. There she is called a prophetess, Aaron's sister. In Num 12:1-15 she is involved in a controversy over Moses' Cushite wife, according to one tradition, and over oracular authority, according to another tradition. As a result of the confrontation she is struck with leprosy.

Aside from these two texts, Miriam is included in only five verses of Scripture. She appears in Mic 6:4 as mentioned above. She is called the sister of Moses and Aaron in the Levitical genealogies of Num 26:59 and 1 Chr 5:29. Deut 24:9 is a second witness to her leprosy (cf. Num 12). And, according to Num 20:1, she died and was buried at Kadesh.[2]

---

[1] All translations of the biblical texts quoted in this work are from the Revised Standard Version (RSV) as found in *The New Oxford Annotated Bible with the Apocrypha,* 2nd ed. (H. G. May and B. M. Metzger, eds.; New York: Oxford, 1977). Where there is a difference between the enumeration of the MT and the RSV, the Hebrew enumeration is followed as found in *BHK*.

[2] Although popular treatments of Miriam almost always include reference to the part played by the sister of Moses in Exod 2, I shall not

A superficial look at these texts leaves one with little information about Miriam. What, however, does a close examination of the texts show?

THE VIEWS OF BIBLICAL SCHOLARSHIP

At the outset, it might be useful to clarify which secondary works on Miriam will *not* be treated in this section. First of all, commentaries and special studies on the seven individual texts which mention Miriam will be incorporated into the chapters which follow and thus will not be reviewed here. Secondly, short articles on Miriam which appear in Bible dictionaries will not be reviewed since, generally speaking, one finds there merely a summary of what is said about Miriam in the biblical texts. Finally, I shall not review the portrait of Miriam which is found in numerous popular studies on biblical figures since this modern *haggadah* is generally not founded on a critical approach to the Scriptures.[3]

Leaving aside the above-mentioned works, a survey of exegetical studies on the biblical portrait of Miriam will, of necessity, be brief since very little has been written on this subject. When she is considered in scholarly works, the attention given to Miriam generally ranges from less than one sentence to only a paragraph or two.

Miriam is mentioned in some works which deal with the role of women in Hebrew religious thought and practice and, more generally, in some works which deal with Hebrew religion and culture. When she is considered in these works, the quest is usually to determine her role in ancient Israel. Scholarly attention naturally focuses on the two longest texts which mention her, Exod 15:20-21 and Num 12. The five remaining texts are rarely, if ever, brought into a scholarly consideration of her role in the Hebrew community. She is frequently mentioned in commentaries on these texts but the focus of those treatments is not on Miriam or her role.

---

include that text in my study. Both the legendary character of Exod 2 (see, e.g., Noth, *Exodus: A Commentary* [OTL; Philadelphia: Westminster, 1962] 26-27 and the treatment by J. P. Hyatt, *A Commentary on Exodus* [NCB; London: Marshall, Morgan and Scott, 1971] 62) and the fact that Moses' sister there is not named prevent me from identifying this figure with Miriam.

[3]For an interesting study of the portrait of Miriam in ancient Jewish *haggadah* and its relationship to the portrait of Mary in the New Testament, see R. Le Déaut, "Miryam, soeur de Moïse, et Marie, mère du Messie," *Bib* 45 (1964) 198-219.

Scholarly discussion on Miriam centers on her as a prophetess and as a cult figure. In recent literature, Phyllis Bird and Clarence Vos have recognized the difficulty of the prophetess designation. While Bird merely mentions the problem in a footnote (" . . . the meaning of the term in this early period is disputed"),[4] Vos gives some attention to it.[5] He concludes that she is not to be regarded as representing ecstatic prophecy. Rather, he says, the designation probably reflects a view of Miriam as "one who speaks for God" although, as he points out, this role is not substantiated by biblical accounts of her activity. Vos would not go so far as to say that the title is anachronistic.[6] His view of Miriam as prophetess can be summarized as follows:

> With respect to Miriam it is possible that the term *prophetess* had a rather broad meaning indicating little more than that she was a leader (possibly a leader or teacher among women as Ex. 15:20 may suggest) in Israel, and that no specific function is indicated by the word.[7]

Miriam appears in a chapter entitled "Women in the Cult" in John Otwell's recent book on the status of women in the OT. Otwell's treatment of Miriam's place in Israel's cult is limited to a single sentence: "Miriam and Deborah are . . . described as cult singers (Exod 15:20f.; Judg 5:12)."[8] Phyllis Bird points to Miriam's appearance alongside Aaron as evidence that she was a cult figure.[9] In a footnote Bird adds that Miriam's

---

[4]P. Bird, "Images of Women in the Old Testament," in *Religion and Sexism: Images of Women in the Jewish and Christian Traditions* (ed. R. R. Ruether; New York: Simon and Schuster, 1974) 85, n. 76.

[5]C. J. Vos, *Woman in Old Testament Worship* (Delft: Judels & Brinkman, 1968) 175-178.

[6]Ibid., 191.

[7]Ibid., 183.

[8]J. H. Otwell, *And Sarah Laughed: The Status of Women in the Old Testament* (Philadelphia: Westminster, 1977) 158. Otwell (173) refers to Miriam again in a later paragraph on cultic singers. I hope to show in chapter 2 that Otwell is incorrect in drawing an analogy between Miriam's and Deborah's songs and the women's chant recorded in 1 Sam 18:7. The latter is not cultic at all.

[9]Bird, "Images of Women in the Old Testament," 68.

leprosy " . . . in which she is made cultically unclean and excluded from the holy camp, also suggests a cultic interpretation of her role."[10]

Some see a connection between the designation of Miriam as prophetess and Miriam as a cult figure.[11] Pedersen views Miriam as a "female element in the personnel of the cultus" and, pointing to the prophetess designation in Exod 15:20, says that "she is then to be sought among the prophets of the temple" and that " . . . she conducts the dances performed by the women" at Passover.[12] Peritz views Miriam primarily as a prophetess and seeks to determine the meaning of this term in the early period by turning to (1) the figures of Deborah and Samuel, (2) 1 Sam 9:9 where "prophet" is equated with "seer," and (3) to a parallel with the role of the Arabic seer-priest (kâhin). Having begun with the figure of Miriam as prophetess in Num 12, Peritz concludes:

> While the incident thus brings out Moses' preeminence, it at the same time asserts the official equality of Miriam with Aaron. That the whole incident is brought into intimate connection with the אֹהֶל מוֹעֵד, the centre of the religious cult, is certainly significant. If to this be added the facts, that occasion is taken to state that Miriam is the sister of Aaron (Ex. 15:20), and that in the earlier genealogical list her descent is traced back to Levi (Nm. 26:59; 1 Chr. 6:3; Ex. 6:20 [P] does not mention her), while throughout she is associated with Aaron and Moses as a leader of the religious community, the conclusion can scarcely be avoided that, as Deborah like Samuel, so Miriam like Moses and Aaron, is an example of a seer in whom, in the manner of that time, the functions of prophet and priest are combined. The probability of this inference is heightened, if in this connection again we call to mind the activity of prophetesses in other Semitic

---

[10]Bird, "Images of Women in the Old Testament," 85, n. 76.

[11]Otwell (And Sarah Laughed, 158) treats Miriam as prophetess under the chapter heading "Women in the Cult," although it is not clear whether he views the prophetess role as cultic. Vos (Women in Old Testament Worship, 191) recognizes that the activity of Miriam described in Exod 15:20 belongs to the realm of Israel's worship but he is doubtful that there is a connection between the worship situation described there and the prophetess designation.

[12]J. Pedersen, Israel: Its Life and Culture (4 vols.; London: Oxford University, 1940), 3-4, 166-167.

religions, and woman's part as diviner in connection with the
oracles later proscribed by the religion of Jahveh.[13]

Finally, Martin Noth includes Miriam in a section, "Figures Alongside
of Moses" in *A History of Pentateuchal Traditions*. Unlike the works cited
above, Noth undertakes a traditio-historical approach to the biblical
portrait of Miriam. The designation of Miriam as prophetess leads him to
suggest that Miriam was a southern Judean colleague of Deborah.[14] He
regards the relationship of Miriam and Aaron as belonging to "now insol-
uble problems,"[15] although he does suggest that Aaron and Miriam were
related as brother and sister in the tradition prior to the brothers-sister
relationship of Aaron, Moses and Miriam.[16] The text in Micah 6 which
links the three is regarded as a late passage by Noth.[17] Numbers 12, he
says, is also late and reflects " . . . a polemic that is no longer under-
standable to us."[18] Finally, Noth regards the notice of Miriam's death in
Num 20:1 as a late text and one which "is completely eliminated as a
possible contribution of an old Miriam tradition."[19] In sum, Noth says of
Miriam:

---

[13]I. Peritz, "Woman in Ancient Hebrew Cult," *JBL* 17 (1898) 144.
Peritz's argument and conclusion were echoed by Caroline Breyfogle, "The
Religious Status of Woman in the Old Testament," *Biblical World* 35 (1910)
405-419. However, the method whereby Peritz reached his conclusions
must be questioned. First of all, I shall attempt to demonstrate in chapter
3 that it is erroneous to view the role of Miriam in Numbers 12 as that of
a prophetess. Secondly, I shall argue that the "prophetess" designation of
Miriam in Exod 15:20 is anachronistic and hence cannot necessarily be
equated with the role of seer. Finally, although the biblical portraits of
Miriam and Deborah bear some similarities, there are also significant
differences (e.g., the Bible records prophetic activity on Deborah's part
but none for Miriam) which prohibit me from defining Miriam's role on an
analogy to that of Deborah. Although my study will show that Miriam was
portrayed as having had a cultic function in ancient Israel (and I shall
consider whether or not this was priestly in character), this conclusion is
not warranted by the "prophetess" material.
[14]M. Noth, *A History of Pentateuchal Traditions* (Englewood Cliffs,
N.J.: Prentice-Hall, 1972) 182.
[15]Ibid., 181.
[16]Ibid., 178, n. 499, and 218.
[17]Ibid., 157, n. 448.
[18]Ibid., 182.
[19]Ibid., 183. Noth later changed his views on the date of Num 20:1. See
his *Numbers: A Commentary* (OTL; Philadelphia: Westminster, 1968) 145.

. . . lacking any other plausible derivation, it is highly probable that behind the figure of Miriam stands a historical person. The only thing is that neither geographically, chronologically, nor historically can we establish more precisely her proper place.[20]

This survey of views on the biblical portrait of Miriam shows that scholarly results on the question have been in proportion to attempts to study the figure in depth. The attention given to such a study has been minimal, as have been the results.

THE PRESENT TASK

Noth's pessimistic views on the possibility of saying anything at all about Miriam, together with his suggestion that "at one time much more was told about her which is now completely lost"[21] form the challenge which gave rise to the present study. Since no one has yet undertaken a detailed examination of the texts with a view to finding what they say about this biblical figure, Noth's conclusion might be viewed as premature.

The present task, then, is this: does a close study of the seven tests which mention Miriam yield more than biblical scholars have concluded about her up to now? Is it not possible to recover more of the biblical portrait of Miriam?

At the outset I wish to make clear that this study is not a "quest for the historical Miriam." I do hold to the probability that the biblical figure of Miriam somehow had roots in the memory of an historical person; however, it is commonly recognized that biblical personalities often took on new and different characteristics as their memories were passed on from age to age. So, although in the course of this study I shall raise some possibilities regarding the historical starting point of the biblical portrait of Miriam, my primary aim is to characterize the tradition's view of Miriam and not to establish the historical facts about her.

The nature of the task is synthetic, i.e., the goal is to arrive at a characterization of the overall biblical portrait of Miriam which can be

---

[20]Noth, *Pentateuchal Traditions,* 182.

[21]Ibid., 182. In 1910 Caroline Breyfogle ("Woman in the Old Testament," 414) voiced the same suggestion this way: Miriam "may have been more prominent in history than tradition was allowed to represent in an age characterized by man's dominance over woman."

gleaned from the individual textual witnesses about her. However, because virtually none of the texts which mention Miriam have been the subject for detailed scholarly analysis, and because none have been studied with my particular goal in mind, it is necessary first of all to clearly establish the character of each of the individual pieces of the portrait. This is what I shall attempt to do in chapters 2, 3, 4 and 5.

The subject of chapter 2 is the account of Miriam's celebration (Exod 15:20-21). I hope to show that the dance, song and playing of the timbrel attributed to Miriam were ritual actions characteristically used in Israel's celebrations in honor of the Divine Warrior. In representing Miriam as leading this celebration, an early writer portrayed a religious and cultic leader, although an account of her rise to such a position is conspicuously absent. At an early stage of tradition, then, Miriam was portrayed as a leader in the pre-Conquest community and the sphere for her activity was the cult.

In chapter 3, I shall examine the biblical witness that Miriam was a prophetess. My study of the prophetess designation which appears in Exod 15:20 shows that, although Miriam was called a prophetess, she is not represented as conducting any specifically prophetic activity. The prophetess designation then, is probably best regarded as an anachronism. This indicates that those scholars who have used the prophetess designation of Exod 15:20 to interpret Miriam's role in Num 12:1-15 are on uncertain ground. But if Numbers 12 does not witness to Miriam's prophetic role, what does it say about her?

More than one level of tradition is present in Num 12:1-15. In the controversy of vv 2-9 Miriam is portrayed as one who claimed authority in rendering God's word. In doing so she voiced the concerns of a priestly, not a prophetic group. The story did not deny her claim but merely established the superiority of Moses in this regard. Miriam, then, is presented as one who authentically rendered God's word although her authority in doing so was subordinate to that of Moses.

Num 12:2-9 has been conflated with an earlier story in which Miriam confronted Moses over his Cushite wife and consequently was struck with leprosy (Num 12:1, 10ff.). Viewing this tradition alongside other "murmuring" texts in the wilderness narratives, one can surmise that in raising the issue alluded to in Num 12:1, Miriam was represented as voicing a community concern and not a personal one. So understood, Numbers 12, like Exod 15:20-21, portrays Miriam as a leader in the community.

In an attempt to harmonize the two stories, Aaron was introduced into the earlier story (Num 12:1, 10ff.). This addition specifically rendered Miriam's leprosy as a case of ritual uncleanness, thus pronouncing her

unfit as a (cultic?) mediator between God and community. The end of the
unit, however, shows that this was a temporary punishment. Her rein-
statement in the community is specifically presented as an act of divine
clemency.

In chapter 4, I shall examine the texts which say that Miriam was the
"sister" of Aaron and Moses (Exod 15:20; Num 26:59; 1 Chr 5:29). In linking Miriam to Aaron and Moses by the use of kinship terminology, the
texts portray Miriam as a religious leader alongside the two. As "sister,"
she is equal to the two in religious leadership although her and Moses'
subordination to Aaron in the priesthood is clear. I suggest that while it is
possible that Miriam functioned in a priestly capacity, the texts do not
firmly cast her portrait as that of priestess. Indeed, it appears that no
such model was available to writers of the monarchical period and later.

In my view the designation of Miriam as Aaron's sister (Exod 15:20)
represents part of a late effort to relate Aaron to early cultic officials.
Subsequently Miriam was included in the genealogies as "sister" to both
Aaron and Moses. Prior to the tradition of this kinship filiation, however,
Miriam appears to have held a prominent position in Israel's religious
tradition which was independent of her "brothers."

In chapter 5, I shall present my analysis of the three remaining texts
which mention Miriam. Deut 24:8-9 sheds little light on her biblical portrait. It does, however, help to date some of the material in Numbers 12
and it supports the witness of other texts that Miriam was remembered as
belonging to the wilderness period.

The mention of Miriam in Mic 6:4 likewise confirms the Pentateuchal
witness that Miriam was a leader alongside Moses and Aaron during the
wilderness period. This text is the only one to explicitly say that she was
divinely commissioned in such a role.

The notice of Miriam's death and burial at Kadesh (Num 20:1b) appears
to be an authentic tradition. If the biblical portrait of Miriam had roots in
the memory of an historical person, the notice of Num 20:1b suggests that
the starting point for her portrait in the tradition was Kadesh.

Having outlined the contributions of the individual texts regarding the
portrait of Miriam, I shall in my concluding chapter, offer my characterization of the composite portrait of her which the individual texts, taken
together, suggest. The overall portrait, simply stated, is this: Miriam was
a leader in the Israelite community who belonged to the wilderness period.
As a leader she was connected with a mediatorial role which was specifically religious in character. The texts suggest a dual aspect regarding the
sphere of her leadership: she was an official in the cult and one who
authentically rendered God's word to the community. By synthesizing the

results of chapters 2 through 5, drawing first from one and then from another, I shall attempt to show in chapter 6 how my characterization of the biblical portrait of Miriam is warranted by the results of my analysis of the individual texts.

ETYMOLOGY

Before turning to the texts, I digress very briefly to examine the meaning of Miriam's name.

The exact etymology of *miryām* is uncertain. The rabbis understood the name to be derived from the Hebrew root *mrr*, "to be bitter."[22] This derivation, however, is unlikely since the particular form of Miriam's name does not represent any known form of this root in the Hebrew. Likewise, Bardenhewer's suggestion that Miriam's name means "the plump one" (from the root *mr*ʾ, "to be fat") and Bauer's suggestion that it means "wished-for child" (from the Arabic *maram*, "wish" or "wished-for") have not been well received.[23]

It appears most probable that the name is to be traced to a form of the Egyptian *mer*, "love." The Egyptian form, *mry(t)* ("the beloved") is commonly found in Egyptian records in combination with the name of a deity, e.g., *mry(t) pth* ("Beloved of Ptah"), *mry(t) r*ʾ ("Beloved of Re"), *mry(t) ʾimn* ("Beloved of Amon").[24] In 1906 Zorell suggested that Miriam's name represents a combination of this Egyptian root and *Yam*, the latter being viewed by Zorell as a Hebrew form of the name of Yahweh.[25] However, because there is little evidence to suggest that the God of the Hebrews was ever called Yam and because it is unlikely that Miriam's name represents a combination of both an Egyptian and a Hebrew word, Zorell's

---

[22]See s. v. "Miriam" by J. F. Ross in *IDB*. C. H. Gordon (*Ugaritic Manual* [AnOr 35; Rome: Pontifical Biblical Institute, 1955] 292) has shown that in some Ugaritic and biblical texts this root also means to "strengthen, bless, commend." See the insightful use of Gordon's discovery by J. M. Sasson, "Numbers 5 and the 'Waters of Judgment,'" *BZ* 16 (1972) 249-51.

[23]For Bardenhewer's position and a critique, see A. H. Gardiner, "The Egyptian Origin of Some English Personal Names," *JAOS* 56 (1936) 195. H. Bauer's work is "Die Gottheiten von Ras Shamra," *ZAW* 51 (1933) 87, n. 2 and *ZAW* 53 (1935) 59.

[24]See Gardiner, "Egyptian Origin," p. 195 and especially Paul Humbert, "Der Name Meri-baʿal," *ZAW* 38 (1919-20) 86.

[25]F. Zorell, "Was bedeutet der Name Maria?" *ZKT* 30 (1906) 356-360.

suggestion that Miriam's name means "Beloved of Yahweh" is less than convincing. Another attempt to explain Miriam's name was advanced in 1952 by Hösl.[26] He suggested that the name represents a combination of the Egyptian *mry (mrj)* plus *ʾimn* (Amon). Thus, he suggested, Miriam's name is to be understood as meaning "Beloved of Amon." Here again, however, it seems to be pressing the evidence to see in the final *mem* of Miriam's name the name of the Egyptian god Amon.[27]

The Egyptian witness of several names combining *mry* (from *mer*) and the name of a deity suggests that the best explanation of Miriam's name is to view it as derived from the Egyptian word meaning "Beloved." If this is correct, it appears likely that at one time her name included that of a deity ("Beloved of X") although the name of the deity has been lost. The Egyptian etymology of Miriam's name is strengthened by the commonly accepted view that the name of Moses, too, has roots in the Egyptian as do names of other early figures (e.g., Hophni, Phinehas). Although some have viewed the Egyptian etymology of Moses' name as evidence for the authenticity of the tradition that he was born and raised in Egypt, the Amarna letters indicate that Egyptian influence was widespread in the ancient Near Eastern world of the fourteenth century B.C. Therefore, one need not conclude from the proposed etymology that Miriam was raised in Egypt. Furthermore, since there is no evidence in the Egyptian records that names beginning with *mry* belonged characteristically or exclusively to any particular group or class, one can conclude that Miriam bore a name common in the Egyptian tongue.

---

[26]I. Hösl, "Zur orientalischen Namenkunde: Maria-Moses-Aaron: eine philologische Studie" in *Serta Monacensia: Franz Babinger zum 15. Januar 1951 als Festgruss dargebracht* (ed. H. J. Kissling and A. Schmaus; Leiden: Brill, 1952) 80-83.

[27]M. Noth (*Die israelitischen Personennamen im Rahmen der gemein-semitischen Namengebung* [Hildesheim: Georg Olms, 1966] 60) prescinds from the question of the etymology of Miriam's name. He simply notes the tendency in later periods to name persons after figures in early Israelite history. Miriam therefore became a popular name in late Judaism.

2

Miriam's Celebration
(Exodus 15:20-21)

A great deal of scholarly attention has been given to the Song at the Sea as recorded in Exod 15:1-18. The discussion has largely centered on questions of the song's date, its literary unity, and its use in cult. The concern in this chapter is, to a large extent, tangential to that discussion. Herein the alternate tradition of the celebration as recorded in Exod 15:20-21 shall be viewed. The text is as follows:

> Then Miriam, the prophetess, the sister of Aaron, took a timbrel in her hand; and all the women went out after her with timbrels and dancing. And Miriam sang to them:

> "Sing to the Lord, for he has triumphed gloriously; the horse and his rider he has thrown into the sea."

Exod 15:20-21 is generally given passing reference in secondary works which deal with Exod 15:1-18, victory celebrations, and dance in the Hebrew scriptures. Admittedly, the brevity of the text and its relative isolation offer little in the way of stimulus for scholarly discussion. However, a study of the portrait of Miriam in the Hebrew scriptural tradition demands that the text be treated at some length.

I shall begin my analysis of this text by citing noteworthy elements in the text of Exod 15:20-21 and by discussing its relationship to Exod 15:1-18 and the narrative sources.

The central portion of this chapter will be focused on the rituals which are attributed to Miriam in Exod 15:20-21. I hope to show that the celebration which she led was essentially a cultic one. That this is so is suggested by the fact that the victor at the sea was Israel's Divine Warrior and not a human one. The essentially cultic nature of Miriam's celebration is confirmed by an examination of the use of dance and song in other

cultic victory celebrations.[1] My examination of related texts will entail
(a) showing that the texts reflect cultic situations, (b) showing that the
cultic situations under examination are victory celebrations honoring
Yahweh and (c) showing that dance and song as ritual actions in these
contexts were intended as symbolic re-presentations of the saving action
of the Divine Warrior. In addition I shall briefly offer an analogy which
may shed light on Miriam's playing of the timbrel.

Although the central section of this chapter appears to go far afield
from a study of the biblical portrait of Miriam, it is intended to provide
the proper context in which Miriam's celebration must be understood. My
study will show that an early stage of the tradition firmly connected
Miriam with Israel's cult.[2] This and other conclusions regarding what a
proper understanding of this text contributes to the biblical portrait of
Miriam will be stated in the final section of the chapter.

The description of Miriam as prophetess and as Aaron's sister will be
treated at length in other chapters and hence will be overlooked here.

THE EXODUS 15:20-21 TEXT

Exod 15:20-21 is virtually free of textual difficulty. Both LXX and Vg
read the Hebrew plural imperative at the beginning of the song as a
cohortative ("Let us sing") but the variants do not bear any change in the
meaning. Likewise, the LXX reads a simple participle for the participle
with suffix (rōkĕbô) which appears in the MT, but again, no change of
meaning is indicated by the variant.[3]

Two elements of Exod 15:20-21 clearly indicate that Miriam was
regarded as the leader of the women in the celebration: (1) "all the women
went out after her," and (2) "she sang to them."[4] The fact that Miriam's

---

[1] Since the rituals of victory celebrations and their meaning are relatively unexplored territory in scholarly circles, considerable attention
must be given to them.

[2] In chapter 4 it will be seen that this early view of Miriam led later
generations to refer to her as Aaron's "sister."

[3] F. M. Cross, Jr. (*Canaanite Myth and Hebrew Epic* [Cambridge:
Harvard University, 1973] 127, n. 48) and S. Mowinckel ("Drive and/or
Ride in O.T.," *VT* 12 [1962] 278-99) note that cavalry was not used in
Egyptian warfare until much later. Consequently, both suggest that the
phrase here must refer to war chariots drawn by horses.

[4] "To them" here is actually a masculine form in the Hebrew. However,
on the frequent use of masculine suffixes (especially in the plural) refer-

part in the celebration is clearly distinguished from that of the rest of the women might well reflect an antiphonal recitation of the song, as some have suggested.[5] This is supported by the use of the verb watta‘an ("and she sang"), which has a fundamental nuance of "reply,"[6] and by the antiphonal character of the longer hymn, Exod 15:1-18.[7]

According to Exod 15:1 the celebration belonged to "Moses and the sons of Israel" but in Exod 15:20 it is Miriam who led "all the women" in the celebration. Many have suggested that Exod 15:20 is the older of the two traditions.[8] Cross and Freedman opt for the superiority of the tradition which associates the celebration with Miriam:

> It is easy to understand the ascription of the hymn to the great leader. It would be more difficult to explain the association of Miriam with the song as a secondary development.[9]

Noth[10] says that the song was attributed to Moses because of the use of the first person singular in the first line of the hymn (Exod 15:1).

The relationship of the song in Exod 15:21 to that of Exod 15:1 has been a point of discussion for many.[11] The discussions have, for the most part,

---

ring to feminine substantives, see GKC 440. Cf. 389ff. on the gender of Hebrew nouns and especially 391 on the masculine as the prior gender in Hebrew.

[5]See, e.g., Noth, Exodus, 122, and J. Blenkinsopp, "Ballad Style and Psalm Style in the Song of Deborah: A Discussion," Bib 42 (1961) 63.

[6]BDB, s. v. ‘nh. The same Hebrew word is used of the women's singing to Saul and David in 1 Sam 18:7, 21:12 and 29:5, and of the singing before the golden calf in Exodus 32.

[7]On the antiphonal character of Exod 15:1-18 see H. Schmidt, "Das Meerlied: Ex. 15:2-19," ZAW 49 (1931) 59-66; M. Rozelaar, "The Song of the Sea (Exodus XV, 1b-18)," VT 2 (1952) 221-28; F. M. Cross and D. N. Freedman, "The Song of Miriam," JNES 14 (1955) 237-50; Blenkinsopp, "Ballad Style," and literature cited therein. Mowinckel (The Psalms in Israel's Worship, [2 vols.; Oxford: Basil Blackwell, 1962], 2. 82ff.) says that in cultic singing in Hebrew circles the leadership role and the "congregational " response were differentiated from earliest times through Temple worship.

[8]See the paragraph which follows and sources cited there.

[9]Cross and Freedman, "The Song of Miriam," 237.

[10]Noth, Exodus, 123.

[11]The lines are identical except for the fact that the verb in 15:1 appears in the singular cohortative ("I will sing") while in 15:21 the form is

focused on the question of dating. Schmidt summarized the positions set
forth prior to the publication of his article in 1931. There he says that
answers to the question fall into two categories: (1) that the longer song
introduced by Exod 15:1 is earlier and Miriam's song in Exod 15:21 is an
abbreviation of it (Holzinger, Kautzsch, Nöldeke, Mowinckel); (2) that
Miriam's song is the original and was elaborated (Exod 15:1-18) by a later
hand for use in the cult (Gunkel, Hinneberg, Kittel, Grossmann, Staerk,
Eissfeldt and Hempel).[12] Since 1931, scholarly opinion has fallen largely
in line with earlier views which opt for the priority of Exod 15:21.[13] But
in an article which is largely devoted to demonstrating the early origin of
Exod 15:1-18, Cross and Freedman write:

> The opening verse also served as the title of the song in
> antiquity, in accordance with standard practice in titling
> poems. Hence v. 21 is not a different or shorter or the origi-
> nal version of the song, but simply the title of the poem taken
> from a different cycle of traditions.[14]

Pace Cross and Freedman, Miriam's song does not necessarily presuppose
the longer hymn. First of all, the fact that its doublet in Exod 15:1 stands
outside the strict strophic pattern of the rest of the longer hymn would
seem to indicate this.[15] Secondly, the amazing ability of the two-line
stanza to survive as a formal unit is clearly indicated in the scriptures. It

---

plural imperative. J. Muilenberg ("A Liturgy on the Triumphs of Yahweh,"
Studia Biblica et Semitica [Vriezen Volume; Wageningen, 1966] 238) cites
the use of the singular cohortative in similar song openings in ancient
Near Eastern practice. The use of the plural imperative (as in 15:21) is
much more common in Hebrew invitations to praise (see, e.g., Pss 47, 81,
96, 98, 100, etc.) and, according to Cross (*Canaanite Myth and Hebrew
Epic*, 127, n. 47) is preferable. Mowinckel (*Psalms*, 2. 83) says that, as a
rule, songs were intoned by a leader. This might explain the use of the
first person in 15:1.

[12]Schmidt, "Das Meerlied," 59. Schmidt sees not two but three units in
Exod 15:1-21. He couples v 1 with v 19 and sets them apart from the hymn
in vv 2-18. Vv 20-21 comprise a third unit.

[13]E.g., Noth, *Exodus*; Blenkinsopp, "Ballad Style"; Rozelaar, "Song of
the Sea"; and J. C. Rylaarsdam, "The Book of Exodus," in *IB* 1. 833-1099.

[14]Cross and Freedman, "The Song of Miriam," 237. It is clear that
Cross and Freedman are reacting against earlier scholarship which too
easily equated "short" with "early."

[15]Rozelaar, "Song of the Sea," 226.

is remarkable that two-line chants connected in one way or another with battle seem to have been especially prone to circulate independently. This is evidenced by the fact that the song of Exod 15:21 (= 15:1) was recorded by variant traditions. The two-line chant of the women who greeted Saul and David is recorded in three different contexts (1 Sam 18:7; 21:12; 29:5). The same is true of the Levites' war song (2 Chr 20:21; cf. 2 Chr 7:3 and Psalm 136). The song before the Ark (Num 10:35) recurs in Ps 68:2 and Ps 132:8. Finally, although Albright's atomizing of thirty or more incipits in Psalm 68 has not been well accepted,[16] it is widely agreed that behind the psalm stand several short and originally independent war songs.[17] Thus, those who say that victory songs were originally short, two-line stanzas repeated indefinitely might well be correct.[18]

The brevity of Exod 15:20-21 and its relative isolation from the sur- rounding narratives make it difficult to assign to one or another of the epic traditions. Because it is generally recognized as old and because of some affinities which it has with the J account in Exodus 14, it is often tentatively assigned to the J source.[19]

Exod 15:20-21 is, then, without significant textual difficulty. There are good reasons for regarding it as the older of the two traditions which

---

[16]W. F. Albright, "A Catalogue of Early Hebrew Lyric Poems (Psalm LXVIII)," *HUCA* 23 (1950) 1-37. Mowinckel's study, *Der achtundsechzigste Psalm* (Oslo: I Kommisjon hos Jacob Dybwad, 1953) 1-78, was written as a refutation of Albright's thesis on Psalm 68. Mowinckel, however, went to the opposite extreme, finding Psalm 68 to be a perfect unity with a *Sitz im Leben* in the New Year's enthronement festival. This, at least, is the view offered by P. D. Miller, Jr., *The Divine Warrior in Early Israel* (Cam- bridge: Harvard University, 1973) 102-3.

[17]See, e.g., Miller, *Divine Warrior,* 103-4, and references cited there.

[18]See, e.g., Mowinckel, *Psalms* 1. 26, and the citation there of similar practices in other societies; see also O. Eissfeldt, *The Old Testament: An Introduction* (New York: Harper and Row, 1965) 100. Other examples of short victory songs include Ps 118:15-16 where a song of victory is quoted: "Hark, glad songs of victory in the tents of the righteous: 'The right hand of the Lord does valiantly, the right hand of the Lord is exalted, the right hand of the Lord does valiantly!'" Kittel (*BHK*) notes that some manu- scripts delete the last line of this song. Also, see Judg 16:23-24 and pos- sibly Ps 24:8, 10.

[19]Cross ("The Song of Miriam," 238) postulates the E source for Exod 15:20-21. Cf. A. Weiser, *The Old Testament: Its Formation and Develop- ment* (New York: Association, 1961) 116.

record the celebration. It is difficult to assign the text with certainty to one or another of the narrative sources.

MIRIAM'S ACTIONS AS CULTIC RITUAL

Battle was a common phenomenon in the ancient Near Eastern world and, like its neighbors, Israel knew the experience well. It was, no doubt, common for the victors to celebrate their success. Thus, when Jephthah returned from his victory over the Ammonites, the text says:

> Then Jephthah came to his home at Mizpah; and behold, his daughter came out to meet him with timbrels and with dances. (Judg 11:34)

A similar celebration is recorded in 1 Samuel, the occasion there being David's return from his victory over the Philistine:[20]

> As they were coming home, when David returned from slaying the Philistine, the women came out of all the cities of Israel, singing and dancing to meet King Saul, with timbrels, with songs of joy and with instruments of music . . . (1 Sam 18:6; cf. 21:12 and 29:5)

Again, leaving aside the notations that Miriam was a prophetess and Aaron's sister, Exod 15:20-21 reads:

> Miriam . . . took a timbrel in her hand; and all the women went out after her with timbrels and dancing. And Miriam sang to them:

---

[20] 1 Sam 18:6 says that when David returned from slaying the Philistine, the women of all the cities of Israel came to greet *King Saul!* Codex Vaticanus of the LXX deals with this problem by omitting "as they were coming home, when David returned from slaying the Philistine." The problem remains, however, in the accompanying chant: "Saul has slain his thousands, and David his ten thousands." As it stands, this hardly appears to be a complimentary chant for a reception for Saul, though it serves the narrator's purpose of providing a background for Saul's jealousy of David (see 1 Sam 18:8ff.). For two different interpretations of this song, compare S. Gervitz, *Patterns in Early Hebrew Poetry* (Chicago: University of Chicago, 1963), 15-24 and W. M. W. Roth, "The Numerical Sequence x/x + 1 in the Old Testament," *VT* 12 (1962) 300-311.

"Sing to the Lord, for he has triumphed gloriously! The horse
and his rider he has thrown into the sea."

The common elements in Exod 15:20, Judg 11:34 and 1 Sam 18:6 are
clear. In all cases, the celebrations of victory (or celebrations honoring
victorious warriors) belong exclusively to women.[21] In all, timbrels and
dances form at least part of the celebration. In addition, the celebrations
of 1 Samuel and Exod 15:20-21 include a two-line chant. These similarities
indicate that the celebration attributed to Miriam was specifically a
celebration of victory.

Miriam's celebration, however, differs (at least on the surface)[22] from
others. Her actions do not honor a victorious warrior who was a charis-
matic leader in the Hebrew community. Rather, her celebration is in
honor of Yahweh, the Divine Warrior of Israel.

The celebration of the Hebrews' victory over the Assyrians, as recorded
in the book of Judith, shows more clearly the difference between secular
celebrations of victory and those celebrations which must be viewed in a

---

[21]In addition to the examples which follow, see Judg 5:28-30 where it
is the women in particular who await Sisera's return from battle. Also see
2 Sam 1:19-20 for the prominent place of women in celebrations of victory. W. O. E. Oesterley, in *The Sacred Dance* (New York: Macmillan,
1923, 40-41) writes: "There are some grounds for believing that the custom of which the Old Testament speaks was a remnant of what was originally a dance performed by women which had for its object the helping of
the men to gain a victory by means of imitative magic. In the Old Testament there is, of course, no trace of this beyond the fact that the dance
was performed by women." In light of this, see Cant 7:1b.

[22]It might be argued that both Jephthah's and David's victories are part
of a holy war motif in that each warrior ascribes his victory to Yahweh.
See Judg 11:30-32 and 1 Sam 17:45ff. I am aware that one must be careful
not to impose modern distinctions between "secular" and "sacred" on
ancient Hebrew practices. It is difficult to know for sure whether or not
the celebrations of Jephthah's daughter and of the women who went out to
meet David contained sacral elements. Some distinction between what
Miriam did and what these other women did, however, seems warranted by
the fact that the warrior Miriam honored was Divine and by the absence
of any suggestion that the celebrations of Jephthah's daughter and of the
women who greeted David were cultic in character. The witness of the
Book of Judith, on the other hand, does seem to reflect more firmly a
distinction between secular and sacred (non-cultic and cultic) celebrations
of victory.

specifically religious and/or cultic context. Jdt 15:12 says that initially "all the women of Israel gathered to see her, and blessed her, and some of them performed a dance for her." However, immediately the focus is shifted:

> and she [Judith] took branches in her hands and gave them to the women who were with her; and they crowned themselves with olive wreaths, she and those who were with her; and she went before all the people in the dance, leading all the women, while all the men of Israel followed, bearing their arms and wearing garlands and with songs on their lips. (Jdt 15:12b-13)

In the verses which follow, Judith witnesses to the belief that the victory and therefore the praise do not properly belong to her but to Yahweh. Thus, what is described is a religious and specifically cultic (see Jdt 16:18ff.) celebration in Jerusalem of Yahweh's victory. The celebration of victory described in Exod 15:20-21 bears closer resemblance to the passage in Judith than to "secular" victory celebrations described in 1 Samuel and Judges 11. In Exodus 15 it appears that Miriam occupies a role very similar to that of Judith: leading the women in praise of Yahweh on the occasion of victory.

In sum, the similarities between Miriam's activity and that of Jephthah's daughter and the women who greeted David clearly indicate that Miriam's celebration was one of victory. But similarities between the celebrations led by Miriam and Judith show that Miriam's celebration differs from those of Jephthah's daughter and the women in 1 Samuel in that the victor whom Miriam honors is Israel's Divine Warrior. Miriam's celebration, then, is a cultic one. That this is the case is apparent not only because (as in the case of Judith) the victor is the Divinity but also because Miriam's dance and song are specifically cultic actions. That the latter is so can be seen when one views the actions attributed to Miriam alongside other texts.

Miriam's Dance

As is the case in numerous societies, dancing is widely attested as part of ancient Hebrew life. It functioned simply as a natural expression of joy[23] but held a place in religious and cultic life as well.[24] Dancing was part of victory celebrations as was seen in the cases of Jephthah's daughter and the women who greeted David. But celebrations of victory also took place in cultic situations and there dance was commonly part of the ritual.[25] Miriam's victory dance must be viewed alongside other instances of ritual dance as it was used in victory celebrations.

The noisy celebration around the golden calf which is described in Exodus 32 included ritual dance (see Exod 32:19). The cultic context is unmistakable. Vv 1, 4 and 8 indicate that the calf was regarded as a Divinity. V 5a says that an altar was built and v 5b says that the celebration which was to follow was regarded as a feast of Yahweh.

Several elements in the Exodus 32 narrative suggest that the celebration described there was a victory celebration. According to Exod 32:17, Joshua mistakenly interpreted the clamor around the calf in a battle context:

> When Joshua heard the noise of the people as they shouted, he said to Moses, "There is a noise of war in the camp."

---

[23]In Eccl 3:4 dancing appears as the opposite of mourning (cf. Lam 5:15). Several other texts (e.g., Jer 31:4, 13; Ps 30:12) show similar meanings of dance in Hebrew life.

[24]1 Sam 10:5ff. and 1 Kgs 18:26 indicate that dance exercised a distinctive role in the activity of ecstatic prophets. Note also the women's dances at vintage and harvest festivals in Judg 9:27 and 21:19ff. More direct evidence of the intimate connection between dance and cultic activity might be found in the two Hebrew words ḥag and pesaḥ. See the discussion in Oesterley, *The Sacred Dance*, 48ff.; cf. H. J. Kraus, *Worship in Israel* (Richmond, Virginia: John Knox, 1966) 45-46.

[25]In addition to the texts treated below, Judg 16:23ff. says that the Philistine celebration on the occasion of Samson's capture was of a cultic nature. They offered a great sacrifice to Dagon, their god, ate, drank, and "rejoiced." (The Hebrew word for "rejoice" here is śimḥâh, a word commonly used to mean rejoicing in general or as part of a religious festival. But see 1 Sam 18:6, 2 Sam 6:12-14, 1 Chr 15:25, 29 and Jer 31:13 where it appears in connection with dance.) Similarly, 1 Sam 30:16 describes the Amalekites' "eating, drinking and dancing" on the occasion of their victories over the Judeans and the Philistines.

His impression was corrected in the following verse[26] but the fact that the cultic celebration around the calf could easily be taken for the "noise of war" suggests that, at least to the ear, the ritual bore close resemblance to what actually took place on the battlefield. Since the context is unquestionably cultic and since no suggestion of actual battle is given, one must regard the celebration as a rehearsal of battle and not an actual battle. The rehearsal of battle is explained by Aaron's announcement in Exod 32:8: "These are your gods, O Israel, who brought you up out of the land of Egypt." The celebration before the calf, then, like the one which Miriam led, commemorated Yahweh's victory over the Egyptians.

What was the meaning of the dance as it was used in the victory celebration of Exodus 32? Verse 6 juxtaposes the cultic eating and drinking with the peoples' "rising up to play."[27] It has been shown that this may be euphemistic terminology for combat.[28] The Hebrew root in Exod 32:6 is $\d{s}hq$. In Judg 16:25 the same root is used interchangeably with $\acute{s}hq$[29] to describe Samson's performance before his Philistine captors while they were gathered at a victory feast honoring Dagon their god. The root $\acute{s}hq$ is used again in 2 Sam 2:14 as two armies gather for a military contest: "Let the young men rise and play before us."[30] It is striking that in the

---

[26]Exod 32:18 says "It is not the sound of shouting of victory, or the sound of the cry of defeat, but the sound of singing that I hear." The translation here might be misleading. For the three different words of the RSV translation ("shouting," "cry" and "singing") the Hebrew uses only one root, $^c nh$ ("singing"). A key word—one which would differentiate the singing before the calf from the "singing of victory" and the "singing of defeat"—is missing from the text. See Noth, *Exodus*, 249.

[27]Cf. 1 Sam 30:16 and Judg 16:23ff.

[28]F. C. Fensham, "The Battle Between the Men of Joab and Abner as a Possible Ordeal by Battle?" *VT* 20 (1970) 356-57 and the literature cited therein. Also see H. A. Hoffner, Jr., "A Hittite Analogue to the David and Goliath Contest of Champions?" *CBQ* 30 (1968) 220-25.

[29]Such changes in consonants from the harder to the weaker sounds do not entail changes in meaning. See GKC 68.

[30]See Fensham's discussion ("Possible Ordeal by Battle?") of this text. The contest described in 2 Sam 2:14ff. apparently involves an actual combat in which twelve representatives from opposing armies decide the victory. Samson's performance, on the other hand, must be regarded as a re-enactment. The context is cultic and there is nothing in the text to suggest that a decision of victory rested on his performance. He is not even given an opponent! By his ritual performance, Samson is forced to testify that the Philistine war god was mightier than Israel's Divine Warrior.

Chronicler's description of David's dance before the Ark, the root *šḥq* is used in parallel to *rqd*, "dance" (1 Chr 15:29; cf. 2 Sam 6:5). The conclusion to be drawn from this is that the ritual combat (i.e., the "rising up to play") before the calf is to be identified with the dancing which Moses saw when he came down from the mountain.[31]

The ritual around the calf (Exodus 32) has elements in common with the ritual dance before the Ark (1 Chronicles 15; cf. 2 Samuel 6). Scholars generally maintain that the Exodus 32 narrative is a polemic against the "two calves of gold" around which Jeroboam centered the cult at Dan and Bethel (1 Kgs 12:26ff.). Jeroboam set up the calves to counteract his peoples' inclination to worship before the Ark in Jerusalem. In setting up the calves he announced: "Behold your gods, O Israel, who brought you up out of the land of Egypt" (cf. 1 Kgs 12:28; Exod 32:8). The calves of gold, then, might be called surrogate Arks.[32] Yahweh, whose presence the calves and the Ark represented, is worshipped as the one who had defeated the Egyptians.[33]

---

[31]This might also suggest that David's dance before the Ark (at least in the Chronicler's view) also took the form of a dramatic rehearsal of battle.

[32]In choosing a rival symbol for the Ark, Jeroboam selected the cult animal of the Canaanite god, Baal. Baal, of course, is the god of vegetation but he is also the great Divine Warrior of the Ugaritic pantheon. On the similarities between the portrayals of Baal and Yahweh as Divine Warriors, see especially Miller, *Divine Warrior* and Cross, *Canaanite Myth and Hebrew Epic*, pp. 91-144.

[33]F. F. Hvidberg (*Weeping and Laughter in the Old Testament* [Copenhagen, n.p., 1962] 148) says that the "rising up to play" of Exodus 32 refers to the sexual content of the feast. He draws this conclusion, however, on the basis of the bull as a fertility symbol and not on textual evidence. Prowess in love and war are difficult to separate in the ancient Near East, of course, but the absence of any other suggestion of the orgiastic character of the Exodus 32 celebration and the clear indication of its character as a victory celebration suggest that the fertility motif, if present at all, was not dominant here. Likewise, J. R. Porter ("The Interpretation of 2 Samuel VI and Psalm CXXXII," *JTS* 5 [1954] 161-73) is at fault in attempting to interpret David's dance (2 Samuel 6) solely in terms of Michal's childlessness and the fertility rites of ancient Near Eastern coronation festivals. If David's dance was indeed a fertility rite, it is highly unlikely that the narrator would have affirmed it over Michal's objections.

In light of the above, the 2 Samuel 6 account of David's dance on the occasion of the entry of the Ark into Jerusalem might also be examined. The cultic context of the dance in 2 Samuel 6 is evident, for example in the procession, sacrifices and blessings. That this is, at least in part, a victory celebration can also be seen. The Ark is the symbol *par excellence* of Yahweh's presence in war.[34] According to the traditions of 1 Sam 4:1-7:2, the Ark fell into Philistine hands and was placed in the temple of Dagon. The result was the shattering of the Philistine god. Finally, a plague caused the Philistines to release the Ark, and it was brought to Kiriath-jearim. 2 Samuel 6 resumes this narrative.[35] Given this background, the triumphal procession with the Ark might well have symbolized the culmination of Yahweh's victory over the Philistines.[36]

There is other evidence that 2 Samuel 6 is to be viewed as a victory celebration.[37] (1) The note in verse 2 explaining the reference to the "ark of God" explicitly connects it with the "Lord of hosts (Yahweh Sabaoth) who sits enthroned on the cherubim."[38] The war-like character of this title is well known.[39] (2) The sounding of the trumpet and the shouts of verse 15 (together with the dance) are commonly found in other contexts of celebrations of Yahweh's victories.[40] (3) It is commonly held that the celebration described in 2 Samuel 6 bears similarity to that of Psalm

---

[34]The clearest indication of this is found in the response of the Philistines when the Ark was brought into the Hebrew camp: "A god has come into their camp" (1 Sam 4:7). See also Num 10:35-36.

[35]Baale-judah (2 Sam 6:2) is probably another name for Kiriath-jearim. See 1 Chr 13:6.

[36]A. Bentzen ("The Cultic Use of the Story of the Ark in Samuel," *JBL* 67 [1948] 37-53) sees the entire narrative of the Ark in 1 and 2 Samuel as a special Davidic edition of the fundamental tradition of Israel. Thus, he says, the account of the liberation from Philistine oppression was intended to parallel the traditions of the liberation from Egypt.

[37]Blenkinsopp ("Kiriath-jearim and the Ark," *JBL* 88 [1969] 143-56) has argued (unconvincingly) that 2 Sam 6:1 originally introduced an account of a climactic military campaign, the account later being misplaced by cultic exigencies of the present narrative.

[38]See also 1 Sam 4:4.

[39]See Cross, *Canaanite Myth*, 69ff. and Miller, *Divine Warrior*, 136, 138-40 and esp. 145-55. Cross (p. 69) calls this "the liturgical name of the Ark."

[40]See the discussion of the victory song below.

132.[41] The connections with holy war there are clearly present in v 8, the war chant used in connection with the Ark:

> Arise, O Lord, and go to thy resting place, thou and the ark of thy might.[42]

(4) Psalm 24 has also been connected with the liturgy of 2 Samuel 6.[43] Vv 8 and 10 show that Yahweh's prowess in battle was highlighted in this liturgy:

> Who is the king of glory? The Lord, strong and mighty, the Lord, mighty in battle!
> . . .
> Who is this king of glory? The Lord of hosts, he is the King of glory!

Connections with victory might also be found in vv 7 and 9. Cross has shown how these lines bear striking similarity to a passage in the Baal myth, a passage which he fits well within the framework of the battle motif in the Ugaritic texts.[44]

Two schools of scholarship interpret the liturgy of 2 Samuel 6 differently. The *Heilsgeschichte* orientation (e.g., Kraus) regards it as a celebration of the election of David and of Jerusalem. The "myth and ritual" orientation (e.g., Mowinckel) views it as belonging to the feast of Yahweh's kingship celebrated at New Year's.[45] For present purposes it is important to note that a cultic re-enactment of victory fits well with either interpretation. Within the *Heilsgeschichte* interpretation, it is significant that David chose the Ark, the palladium of holy war among the tribes, with which to legitimate his own election and that of Jerusalem.

---

[41]See, e.g., Kraus, *Worship in Israel*, 183ff.; A. Weiser, *The Psalms*, OTL (Philadelphia: Westminster, 1962) 780; Mowinckel, *Psalms*, 1. 174-77; and Porter, "2 Samuel VI and Psalm CXXXII." Cf. D. R. Hillers, "Ritual Procession of the Ark and Ps. 132," *CBQ* 30 (1968) 48-55.

[42]Cf. Num 10:35-36 and Cross *Canaanite Myth*, 100.

[43]See, e.g., Mowinckel, *Psalms*, 1. 174-77; Cross, *Canaanite Myth*, 91-99.

[44]Note, however, that Cross's attempt to find exact parallels between the re-enactment of Yahweh's victories and ancient Near Eastern practices led him to conjecture about material which originally lay in lines which are presently missing from the Ugaritic text.

[45]For Kraus's and Mowinckel's treatments, see references in n. 41.

Presumably the rites with the Ark here had affinities with earlier celebrations of the triumphs of Yahweh. The shouts, the sounding of the
trumpets, and the dance would seem to support this. Within the "myth and
ritual" interpretation, one must note that, according to ancient Near
Eastern myth, kingship was won by virtue of victory in battle and kingship
festivals in the ancient Near East commonly included re-enactments of
victory in battle.[46] No doubt the celebration of Yahweh's kingship would
have included the same.

Thus, while 2 Samuel 6 is not ostensibly in a context of holy war, there
does exist sufficient evidence to suggest that at least a subsidiary element in the celebration described there was that of victory.[47]
Admittedly, this element has been blurred in deference to royal ideology.

On the basis of the meaning of the dance as it appears in the victory
celebrations of Exodus 32 and 2 Samuel 6, I suggest that Miriam and the
women's dance as recorded in Exod 15:20 must be understood as a

---

[46]There is widespread evidence of ritual combat in the ancient Near
East. On the tenth day of the Babylonian Akitu Festival, a statue of the
god (Marduk) was carried in procession to a field outside the city and it
was there that Marduk's battle with Tiamat was cultically re-enacted. In
the Akitu-house erected by Sennacherib•in Ashur and in a corresponding
temple in Babylon, pictorial representations of such a "mock battle" have
been found. Similar contests were part of the Hittite kingship festival.
Likewise, the ritual re-enactment of the Osiris drama at the Egyptian
accession festival appears to have contained rather realistic representa-
tions of combat. See H. Ringgren, *Religions of the Ancient Near East,*
(Philadelphia: Westminster, 1973) 29-30, 70, 83-5; A. R. Johnson, "Hebrew
Conceptions of Kingship," in *Myth, Ritual and Kingship* (ed. S. H. Hooke;
Oxford: Clarendon, 1958) 204-35; Pedersen, *Israel,* 3-4. 735; I. Engnell,
Studies in Divine Kingship in the Ancient Near East (Oxford: Basil
Blackwell, 1967) 36, 65-6; A. Erman, *Die Ägyptische Religion,* 2nd ed.
(Berlin: n. p., 1901) 64-5. It is noteworthy that, in all these instances,
ritual combat took place *after* the victory had been won. Thus the rehear-
sal was not so much for the purpose of insuring victory as to celebrate the
new order which the victory established.

Several have posited that Israel, too, celebrated Yahweh's victories
with ritual combat. For example, Pedersen (*Israel, 3-4. 735*) connects
ritual combat with the springtime Passover festival. Mowinckel (*He That
Cometh* [Oxford: Basil Blackwell, 1956] 83) connects it with the autumnal
New Year's festival.

[47]Miller, *Divine Warrior,* 149, agrees.

dramatic re-presentation (as well as a celebration) of Yahweh's victory over the Egyptians at the sea. Several poetic texts support this suggestion. That Isa 30:29-32 reflects a cultic festival is clear from verse 29:

> You shall have a song in the night
> when a holy feast is kept;
> and gladness of heart, as when one sets out
> to the sound of the flute
> to go to the Mountain of the Lord,
> to the Rock of Israel.

The verses which follow indicate that the festival is in honor of the Divine Warrior:

> And the Lord will cause his majestic voice to be heard and the descending blow of his arm to be seen, in furious anger and a flame of devouring fire, with a cloudburst and tempest and hailstones. The Assyrians will be terror-stricken at the voice of the Lord when he smites with his rod.[48]

If Isaiah is envisioning here a festival in honor of the Divine Warrior, what rituals are involved? The continuation of the text says:

> And every stroke of the staff of punishment
> which the Lord lays upon them
> will be to the sound of timbrels and lyres;
> battling with brandished arm
> he will fight them.

The use of song and musical instruments is clear. The specific mention of timbrels together with song in such a context echo Exod 15:20, Judg 11:34, 1 Sam 18:6, etc. In fact, according to v 32a, it seems that the timbrels and lyres are used as musical accompaniment for the violent movements of the Divine Warrior. V 32b suggests that the violent movements took the form of dance. The line in the Hebrew is difficult and the RSV translation might well be improved. The word těnûpâh ("with brandished arm") appears in an adjectival relationship to "battling." Most often

---

[48]On the parallels between the Divine Warrior theophanies of Baal and Yahweh, see Cross, *Canaanite Myth*, 147-77.

the scriptures use *tĕnûpâh* to mean "consecrated," whether referring to offerings of gold or brass for the construction of the tabernacle, the sacrificial portions of the priests, or to the waving gestures with which offerings are made.[49] The word which the adjective modifies in Isa 30:32b is *mīlḥămôt*, "battling" or "battles." However, Kittel suggests that a similar sounding word, *mĕḥōlôt* ("dancing"), be read here. Considering the parallel relationship which this line has to the timbrels and lyres of v 32a, Kittel's suggestion is well founded. Thus, if my own suggestion and that of Kittel are taken,[50] Isa 30:32 reads as follows:

> And every stroke of the staff of punishment
> which the Lord lays upon them
> will be to the sound of timbrels and lyres;
> and with consecrated (cultic) dances
> he will fight them.

What Isaiah envisions bears close similarity to the rituals of other victory celebrations in Israel as they have been studied above.

Finally, and briefly, selections from the psalms shed light on the rituals employed as the victory motif was celebrated in temple worship.

Psalm 149 is a summons to Israel to praise Yahweh, its creator and king. What rituals are reflected there? Dance (v 3a), musical instruments (v 3b), and song (v 5) are all used.[51] Vv 6-9 show that these rituals were employed in the service of the victory motif:

> Let the high praises of God be in their throats
> and two-edge swords in their hands,
> to wreak vengeance on the nations
> and chastisements of the peoples,
> to bind their kings with chains
> and their nobles with fetters of iron,
> to execute on them the judgment written![52]

---

[49]See Exod 29:24, 26; Exod 35:22; Exod 38:24, 29; Num 6:20; Num 8:11ff.; Num 18:11, 18; Lev 8:27; Lev 14:12ff.; Lev 23:15ff.

[50]I would contend that, even without taking Kittel's suggested change in the text, the context (specifically the song and timbrels) offers sufficient evidence for positing the dance as part of the ritual.

[51]See Psalm 150 for the use of instruments and dance in a more general summons to praise.

[52]For Mowinckel these verses suggest a sword dance, similar in function to ritual combats in ancient Near Eastern kingship festivals. See

This suggests that Israel regarded Yahweh's kingship as stemming from a Divine victory over the nations (in a fashion similar to the mythic patterns of Israel's ancient Near Eastern neighbors) and that the celebration of Yahweh's kingship included a dramatization of that victory with the use of musical instruments, song and dance.[53]

Mowinckel regards Psalms 46 and 48 as prominent examples of the "myth about the fight of nations" as it appears in Israel's liturgy.[54] Ps 46:9 ("Come, behold the works of the Lord . . .") is followed by a description of Yahweh's victory over the nations. Ps 48:5-8 describes the flight of the nations before Yahweh and is followed by: "As we have heard, so we have seen in the city of the Lord of hosts . . ." (v 9). On these verses, Mowinckel writes:

> Knowing how thoroughly the cult in ancient times was a "drama" for the purpose of presenting visibly what faith knew to be happening, and considering the prominent part played by ritual fighting games in the cult of ancient peoples, we can hardly help interpreting the words in the above passages as references to ritual acts, through which was presented in a more or less realistic or symbolic way the victory over the united nations.[55]

It is interesting to note the imagery used by the psalmist in describing the defeated kings in Ps 48:7:

> Trembling took hold of them there,
> anguish as of a woman in travail.

Literally, the trembling of kings is likened to the painful writhing of a woman giving birth. That this re-enactment of battle and celebration of victory took the form of dance is supported by the following.

In a study of the portrayal of the Divine Warrior in Canaanite and early

---

Psalms, 1. 181-2, where he related it to the triumphal procession, the center of the enthronement festival of Yahweh.

[53]For the place of the dance (and specifically dancing women) in the cultic procession at the New Year's festival, see Mowinckel, Psalms, 1. 181-2 and Weiser, The Psalms, 489, 724, 729.

[54]Mowinckel, Psalms, 1. 181-2.

[55]Mowinckel, Psalms, 1.181. Cf. Weiser, The Psalms, 372, 382-3.

Hebrew poetry,[56] Frank Moore Cross has pointed out two archaic mythic patterns. In the texts which Cross associates with Pattern I, the Divine Warrior marches forth into battle and, in the face of the Divine wrath, nature writhes and languishes.[57] Texts which Cross associates with Pattern II include a manifestation of the victorious Warrior who, by virtue of victory, is acclaimed king. In response, nature awakens and rejoices.[58] In texts treated by Cross, Patterns I and II are sometimes mixed or conflated. That is to say, in some texts the display of numinous power which accompanies the presence of the Divine Warrior is represented without further specification as to whether it marks a wrathful going forth to battle or a triumphant return. Likewise, conflation occurs in some texts which deal with the awesome response of nature to the appearance of the Warrior. Though the response is not always characterized as fearsome or joyous, it is always violent in intensity.[59]

It should be noted that Patterns I and II which Cross has delineated do not occur in one and the same text. Rather, they are separate categories. There are, however, two connections between the patterns which are significant for purposes of the present study. First of all, Pattern II (the manifestation and celebration of the victor/king) often alludes back to the battle from which the victory and the enthronement arose.[60] Secondly,

---

[56]Cross, *Canaanite Myth*, 91-194.

[57]Cross includes Exod 15:1-18, Hab 3:3-15, Ps 77:15-20, and Psalm 114 in Pattern I. For texts which are partial demonstrations of the pattern, see *Canaanite Myth*, 157.

[58]Texts which Cross includes in Pattern II are Pss 29; 89:6-19; 96; 97:1-6 and 98. For related texts see *Canaanite Myth*, 162.

[59]In Hebrew poetry the fundamentally mythic language has been historicized to a large degree. Thus, for example, the going forth to battle from the sacred mountain (Saphon) becomes Yahweh's march from Egypt or Sinai. Although Cross has worked only with poetic texts, it appears likely that the fundamentally mythic patterns might also be found in narrative accounts of Israel's holy wars. There the language of poetic imagery has been replaced by language which further particularizes Yahweh's action in time and space. In narrative accounts one frequently finds Yahweh (or the Ark) going forth at the head of the Israelite army (not with a heavenly host) in the face of which the enemy's strength collapses into total confusion (Pattern I). Further study might well unearth echoes of Pattern II.

[60]Ps 89:6-19 is a good example. The hymn is primarily one which celebrates Yahweh's might. V 11 refers back to the crushing of Rahab. This element in the pattern is confirmed by extensive ancient Near

the early Hebrew poetic texts which fall into patterns I and II frequently use one Hebrew root, ḥûl (ḥîl)[61] to describe both the writhing of nature in response to the wrathful going forth of the Warrior (Pattern I) and the rejoicing of nature at the victorious return (Pattern II). The Hebrew root means both "to writhe" (as in childbirth) and "to dance."[62]

The mythic patterns which Cross has outlined no doubt were expressed in rituals which were used in Hebrew celebrations of the triumphs of the Divine Warrior. The present examination confirms this. My study shows that dance was a recurring feature in celebrations of victory among the Hebrews. Moreover, it can be seen that, since the victory celebrations were cultic in nature, the dance therein must be regarded as religious ritual. Ritual, properly understood and executed, is never empty. It is symbol. It expresses meaning and keeps it alive.

The victory dance, no doubt, functioned as an expression of joy. However, as ritual it was not an arbitrarily chosen expression. My study indicates that, in some way, the dance in victory celebrations functioned as a rehearsal of the battles of Yahweh. I use the word "rehearsal" loosely. I do not mean a carefully orchestrated dramatic reproduction in which parts are assigned to participants to represent the two sides of combat.[63] Rather, it is likely that the dramatic, violent movements of the dance were sufficient to express at once both the struggle and victory, the pain and exultation, the death and life which battle entails.

Eastern evidence of ritual combat as part of kingship festivals. Cf. n. 46 above.

[61]On middle weak Hebrew roots with similar form and meaning, see GKC 219-20: "The close relation which exists between some classes of the weak verbs . . . appears not only in their similarity or identity of inflexion, or on their mutual interchange of certain forms, but especially from the fact that frequently the same root recurs in various weak stems of similar meaning. The meaning accordingly is inherent in the two constant root-consonants, while the third consonant, which is weak . . . does not establish any difference in the meaning."

[62]BDB s.v. ḥûl. Nouns which derive from this root include those which mean pain, pang, trembling, anguish, power, strength, army and dance.

[63]See Mowinckel's comments (Psalms, 1. 169-70) on the dramatic character of the cultic festival: "The feast is a 'holy drama,' where the contents of the festal myths are presented, and thus are embodied and re-experienced as something which is actually creating what is then coming into existence. Only we must not think that this 'presentation' was anything like a modern realistic play. It is just possible that most of the things 'taking place' were presented by means of suggestive symbols."

Why did the Hebrews repeat in cult the victories of Yahweh once those victories were secured? It is likely that the purpose was to make effective in the present the creation and sustenance of life which past victories accomplished. Noth writes:

> Re-presentation is founded on this—that God and his actions are always present, while man in his inevitable temporality cannot grasp this present-ness except by "re-presenting" the action of God over and over again in his worship.[64]

Finally, why was dance employed to such an end? Van der Leeuw throws light on this when he speaks of the place of the dance in ancient religions:

> . . . the *dance* is not merely an esthetic pursuit existing side by side with other practical activities. It is the service of the god, and generates power: the rhythm of movement has a compelling force. . . . In the dance life is ordered to some powerful rhythm and reverts to its primeval motion, and thus it is possible to attain to all manner of things "by dancing," from one's daily bread to heavenly bliss. There are love-, war-, and hunting dances, which represent *in actu* the desired event, the love union, success in war and hunting.[65]

But in the Hebrew scriptures there are no instances of war dances, i.e., dances which were performed in order to insure victory in battle. There are only dances used in rehearsals of victories already won. As such they have no magical content. They merely express that Yahweh, the insurer of victory in battle is present again, and through ritual actions it is Yahweh who here and now is creating and sustaining life.[66]

----

[64]Noth, "The 'Re-Presentation' of the O. T. in Proclamation," in *Essays on Old Testament Hermeneutics* (ed. C. Westermann; Richmond, Virginia: John Knox, 1963) 85.

[65]G. van der Leeuw, *Religion in Essence and Manifestation* (London: George Allen and Unwin, 1938) 374.

[66]Mowinckel (*Psalms*, 1. 19) describes this phenomenon as "sacramental": "Through the acts and words of the festal cult, laid down in fixed, sacred ritual, the reality which is to be created—the renewal of the herd, of the field, of the forces of life, of righteousness, of blessing and life—is portrayed ('acted') in visual and audible form. The actualization takes place through the representation. This does not mean that the

This study of the place and meaning of dance in cultic celebrations of victory provides the context within which Miriam's dance must be understood. The dance was a standard feature in recurring celebrations honoring the Divine Warrior. As such, it was not merely a simple expression of joy but a cultic re-enactment of the saving action present in the battle itself. In comparing Exod 15:20, then, an early author portrayed Miriam as leading a dance which generations of worshippers would repeat. The prominence given to her by the writer lies not only in the fact that she is the first to so honor Yahweh but also in the fact that the saving action which she ritually re-presented (the deliverance at the sea) was the saving action *par excellence* of Israel's Divine Warrior.

Like the dance of Exod 15:20, Miriam's song is best understood as ritual action.

The Victory Song

The song of Exod 15:21 bears the formal characteristics of a hymn.[67] Thus, the invitation to praise (expressed in the imperative) is followed by *ki* ("for") which in turn introduces a clause which characteristically takes the form of affirmations of Yahweh's character and actions which are worthy of praise. As such, the statement which follows the summons to praise is both the motivation to praise and the praise itself.

Further light on the meaning of Miriam's song as ritual action is offered by an examination of the songs which almost universally accompany the dance in victory celebrations honoring the Divine Warrior. Mowinckel writes:

> The *words* of the cult seem originally to belong to the acts as interpretation and complement—that also being one side of the cult's dramatic character. The power inherent in the act is also concentrated in the word; the holy word is effective

---

representation, the acts and the words, are seen as 'magic' which by itself creates life and renewal. It is the 'powers,' or the deity, Yahweh, who acts and creates through them; to that extent they are 'sacramental.'"

[67]Weiser, *The Old Testament: Its Formation and Development,* 33-4; Eissfeldt, *Introduction,* 107-8; Noth, *Exodus,* 121-22; Muilenberg, "Liturgy," 238. Cf. C. Westermann, *The Praise of God in the Psalms,* (Richmond, Virginia: John Knox, 1965) 89-90. R. H. Pfeiffer, *Introduction to the Old Testament* (New York: Harper and Brothers, 1948) 272, notes the 2.2 meter of Exod 15:21.

and creative. Word and act co-operate in the creation of reality.[68]

If one can posit that dance somehow functioned as a cultic re-enactment of the action on the battlefield, is it also possible to regard the song of victory in the same light, i.e., as somehow re-presenting the shouts which accompanied the action in battle?

According to the scriptures, the actual going forth to engage in battle was often accompanied by a war cry.[69] The Philistines were shouting as they came out to meet Samson (Judg 15:14). David arrived at Saul's encampment against the Philistines "as the host was going forth to the battle line, shouting the war cry" (1 Sam 17:20). And after David's defeat of the Philistine, the men of Israel and Judah "rose with a shout and pursued the Philistines . . ." (1 Sam 17:52). The war cry in these texts simply signalled the engagement of the troops in battle. No particular religious or cultic significance is clearly suggested.

Trumpets were also used in the going forth to battle. There is some suggestion that the purpose of the sounding of the trumpet was not only to sound an alarm for battle but also to designate the battle as a sacral event.[70] The legislation of Num 10 specifically says that the trumpets must be sounded when going to war in order that "you may be remembered before the Lord your God" (Num 10:9). Thus, as Moses sent troops off to fight the Midianites, he sent Phinehas the priest along "with the vessels of the sanctuary and the trumpets for the alarm in his hand" (Num 31:6).

Sometimes trumpets and war cries appear together on the battlefield. The sounding of the trumpets designates the event as sacred (i.e., the presence of the Divinity who is prepared for battle). The war cry no longer signals the engagement of the troops in battle but marks the engagement of the Divinity in battle.[71]

---

[68] Mowinckel, *Psalms*, 1.20.

[69] An extension of the war shout may have been the battle song, a chant used on the battlefield to inspire warriors on to more zealous fighting. Miller (*Divine Warrior*, 94) and P. C. Craigie ("The Song of Deborah and the Epic of Tukulti-Ninurta," *JBL* 88 [1969] 259-60) agree that Judg 5:12 is to be understood as a summons to Deborah to serve such a function in battle.

[70] Cf. the trumpet blasts at Hebrew festivals in Lev 23:24, Lev 25:9 and Num 29:1.

[71] See 1 Sam 4:5: "When the ark of the covenant of the Lord came into the camp, all Israel gave a mighty shout, so that the earth resounded."

In texts which are heavily laden with sacral war motifs, the sounds which once were signals on the battlefield have themselves become effective agents in the victory. According to Judges 7, Gideon's three hundred warriors (presumably not priests as in 2 Chronicles 13 and Joshua 6) were given trumpets and the victory was actually won by the blast of the trumpets and the war cry. Together the two sounds sent the Midianites into utter confusion and they fled. The same phenomenon appears in 2 Chr 20:21. Jehoshaphat sent the Levites before his army and they sang as they went into battle.[72]

> And when they began to sing and praise, the Lord set an ambush against the men of Ammon, Moab and Mount Seir who had come against Judah, so that they were routed. For the men of Ammon and Moab rose against the inhabitants of Mount Seir, destroying them utterly, and when they had made an end of the inhabitants of Seir, they all helped to destroy one another.

Likewise, in Joshua 6 when the trumpet was sounded and the war cry raised, the walls of Jericho fell down flat. Finally, 2 Chr 13:14-15 tells how Jeroboam set an ambush against the army of the southern kingdom:

> And when Judah looked, behold the battle was before and behind them and they cried to the Lord, and the priests blew the trumpets. Then the men of Judah raised the battle shout. And when the men of Judah shouted, God defeated Jeroboam and all Israel before Abijah and Judah.

The only function of the humans in the above narrative is that of supplying the sound (chant and/or trumpet blast) and apparently it was through the medium of those sounds that Yahweh accomplished victory.[73]

What the shout indicated, i.e., that a god had joined the Hebrew forces, left the Philistines terror-stricken.

[72]The Levites' two-line chant in 2 Chr 20:21 is not explicitly related to the battle. The same chant was used in the Temple dedication ceremony according to 2 Chr 7:3. Also cf. Psalm 136. Mowinckel (*Psalms,* 1. 26) is probably correct in saying that "evidently the thanksgiving psalm has its original pattern in the song of victory."

[73]Note the influence of the cult especially in Joshua 6 and 2 chr 20:21. Cross ("The Divine Warrior in Israel's Early Cult," in *Biblical Motifs: Origins and Transformations* [ed. A. Altmann; Cambridge: Harvard Uni-

These texts indicate that as the conventions of secular warfare were permeated by sacral interpretation, their meaning changed. The war cry, once a signal for the engagement of humans in battle, under the influence of the concept of holy war came to be a signal for the engagement of the Divine Warrior in battle. Ultimately, sounds on the battlefield themselves came to be regarded as weapons which accomplished the victory. This development has parallels in the imagery of poetic texts where conventions once used by humans are attributed to the Divine Warrior. Thus, in some texts the war shout, no longer uttered by humans but by the Divinity, signals and is followed by battle. In 2 Sam 22:14-15 (=Ps 18:14-15) one finds:

> The Lord thundered from heaven
> and the Most High uttered his voice.
> And he sent out arrows and scattered them;
> lightning, and routed them.

The same phenomenon appears in Isa 42:13:

> The Lord goes forth like a mighty man,
> like a man of war, he stirs up his fury;
> he cries out, he shouts aloud,
> he shows himself mighty against his foes.[74]

In Ps 104:7 the distinction between the war cry uttered by Yahweh and the actual accomplishment of victory has been blurred:

> At thy rebuke they [the waters] fled;
> at the sound of thy thunder they took to flight.

The clearest and fullest example of the conflation of Yahweh's shout and the actual destruction of the enemy appears in the cosmic imagery of

---

versity, 1966] 26-7) has plausibly suggested that the celebration of ritual conquest lies at the base of the narratives of Josh 3-6. One suspects that the Chronicler has shaped his narrative under the influence of the Temple cult. If this is so, there is little doubt that the narrative arose from Temple celebrations of Yahweh's triumphs.

[74]Cf. D. N. Freedman's translation in "Isaiah 42, 13" in *CBQ* 30 (1968) 225-26. Other examples of the Lord's triumphal shouts appear in Ps 108:10 (= Ps. 60:10), Ps 64:34 and Ps 78:65-66.

Psalm 29, a song which recent scholarship describes as "an ancient Baal hymn, only slightly modified for use in the early cultus of Yahweh."[75] There it is the Lord's voice which breaks the cedars of Lebanon (v 5), shakes the wilderness (v 8), strips the forests bare (v 9), etc.

This phenomenon in the Hebrew traditions of holy war has an analogue in the Assyrian Epic of Tukulti-Ninurta. In that epic, Ishtar is regarded as the Divine Warrior. The decisive turning point in the battle came when "Ishtar smote her lyre which drove their [the enemy's] warriors mad."[76] It is noteworthy that the action of the deity on the battlefield had reverberations in the cult. Haldar cites a cylinder seal which depicts two musician-priestesses playing the harp and the sistrum before Ishtar as she is seated on her lion throne.[77] In addition, the rites of a festival in honor of the Hittite war god included the playing of the "Ishtar instruments" along with other instruments, songs and dance.[78] The worship of Ishtar as Divine Warrior, then, included a cultic repetition of her action on the battlefield. This leads one to ask whether the chants or songs in Hebrew celebrations of victory were intended as cultic re-presentations of the sounds on the battlefield of sacral war.[79]

That song formed an integral part of victory celebrations in Israel is

---

[75]Cross, *Canaanite Myth*, 152. For a discussion of this psalm see the same work, 151-57, 160-62 and the literature cited therein. Miller, (*Divine Warrior*, 35-37) discusses the victory shout uttered by Baal at his enthronement and its parallels with Psalm 29 and 2 Sam 22 (= Psalm 18).

[76]As quoted by Craigie, "Song of Deborah," 260.

[77]A. Haldar, *Associations of Cult Prophets Among the Ancient Semites* (Uppsala: n. p., 1945) 68. On this, see also below, p. 38.

[78]J. B. Pritchard, ed.,*ANET*, 358ff.

[79]The victory song was not always used cultically in the ancient Near East or in Israel. In the Akkadian Epic of Gilgamesh, the hero is greeted in the city of Uruk after his defeat of the Bull of Heaven. The hero himself chants to the lyre-maids: "Who is most splendid among the heroes? Who is most glorious among men?" The maids chant in response: "Gilgamesh is most splendid among the heroes, Gilgamesh is most glorious among men" (*ANET*, 85. See textual notes therein. Also, cf. the antiphonal question-answer in the ritual which stands behind Psalm 24.) Other examples of victory songs from the ancient Near East are cited by J. Gray, *Near Eastern Mythology* (London: Hamlyn Publishing Group, 1969), 79 and Oesterley, *The Sacred Dance*, 163. P. D. Hanson ("The Song of Heshbon and David's *Nîr*," *HTR* 61 [1968], 297-320) regards Num 21:27b-30 as an Amorite victory song borrowed by the Hebrews. See also Gen 4:23-24 and Judg 15:16.

evident.[80] Exod 15:21 is the clearest example of the use of the two-line victory chant. Examples (both early and late) of the use of longer hymns in victory celebrations include Exod 15:1-18, Judges 5 and Judith 16. Of texts reviewed in the preceding section of this chapter, several include reference to songs which accompanied the dance ritual in the cultic re-enactment of Yahweh's victories. Finally, scholars generally recognize that Psalm 68 was used in a celebration of Yahweh's triumphs.[81] In the solemn procession in Psalm 68 one finds "the singers in front, the min-strels last, between them maidens playing timbrels" (v 26).

Other texts treated in connection with the dance suggest that the chants and musical instruments used in cult were closely tied with sounds on the battlefield. For example, it has already been noted that the chant-ing before the calf in Exodus 32 bore enough similarity to the "noise of war" that it was taken as such by Joshua. Ps 132:8 and Ps 68:2 indicate that the chant used with the Ark in holy war ideology (Num 10:35f.) was subsequently used in Temple worship which celebrated the wars of Yahweh.[82] Ps 149:6 ("Let the high praises of God be in their throats and two-edged swords in their hands") suggests that song accompanied a "sword-dance" in a victory celebration. Isa 30:32 says that "every stroke of the staff of punishment which the Lord lays upon them will be to the sound of timbrels and lyres." Following the summons to praise in Ps 47:2-5, the psalmist parallels Yahweh's war shout with temple rituals:

> God has gone up with a shout
> the Lord with the sound of the trumpet.

---

[80]Mowinckel (*Psalms*, 1. 27) writes: "In these songs of victory a reli-gious element very early made itself felt. The festival at the home-coming would naturally be celebrated at the sanctuary (1 Sam. 15:13), where the people used to celebrate other festivals, with both sacrificial slaughter and feasting, which always had a certain cultic character (1 Sam. 14:31ff.). Besides, Israel was always aware that Yahweh himself was at the head of the army of Israel against her enemies and would smite the enemies with terror and death; her wars were the 'wars of Yahweh' (Nm. 21:14), in which the 'heroes came to the help of Yahweh' (Jdg. 5:23). Therefore it is natural that victory would often be described and praised as the great achievement of Yahweh (Ex. 15:21)."

[81]On this problematic psalm, see, e.g., Albright, "Catalogue," Miller, *Divine Warrior*, 102ff.; Mowinckel, *Psalms*, 1. 172ff.; and Weiser, *The Psalms*, 477ff.

[82]Cross, *Canaanite Myth*, 100. Cf. Miller, *Divine Warrior*, 37, where he cites a Ugaritic parallel; also Miller, 145ff. and Mowinckel, *Psalms*, 1. 21.

Sing praises to God, sing praises!
Sing praises to our King, sing praises!

Ps 47:6-7

A similar example is found in Zeph 3:17:

The Lord, your God, is in your midst,
a warrior who gives victory;
he will rejoice over you with gladness,
he will renew you in his love;
he will exult over you with loud singing
as on a day of festival.[83]

Finally, one might recall and return to the archaic mythic patterns in early Hebrew poetry which Cross has demonstrated. In texts which fall into the category which Cross labels Pattern II, nature responds to the manifestation of the Divine Warrior with singing as well as dancing. Thus, for example, in Psalm 98 worshippers are called to praise the Lord with the "joyful noise" of trumpets, horn, lyre and song. Immediately afterward (vv 7-8), nature is summoned to respond in a similar fashion:

Let the sea roar, and all that fills it;
the world and all those who dwell in it!
Let the floods clap their hands;
Let the hills sing for joy together . . .[84]

It is well known that mythic patterns came to expression in cult. My study of texts which show the use of song at victory celebrations confirms this. Songs no doubt functioned as expressions of joy in praise of Yahweh the Divine Warrior. However, as ritual, songs, like the dance, were not arbitrarily chosen expressions. In light of this study cultic victory songs must

---

[83]Cf. also Num 23:21: "The Lord their God is with them, and the shout of a king is among them." Mowinckel (*Psalms*, 1. 122) says that "king" here can be nobody but Yahweh. However, in light of the present study, it seems reasonable to suggest that the war shout might well have been a ritual performed by the reigning king in his capacity as president of the cultic assembly.

[84]Cf. Ps 89:13, where the psalmist says that Tabor and Hermon *sing* their praises.

be viewed as somehow re-presenting the pulsating sounds[85] which accompanied action on the battlefield. Miriam's song of victory, like the others, must be viewed as such.

Before concluding this section on Miriam's actions as cultic ritual, very brief consideration will be given to the use of the timbrel in Miriam's celebration.

Playing the Timbrel

The writer of Exod 15:20 portrayed Miriam as playing a percussion instrument, the timbrel, to facilitate or accompany the rhythm of her dance and chant. Such use of the timbrel (tambourine) is well known from ancient times to the modern day. The Israelites used the timbrel both in cultic and in non-cultic situations, as the texts viewed in this chapter show.

Here I simply wish to call attention to the use of the timbrel in the rituals of ancient Egypt. In his study "On the Position of Women in the Ancient Egyptian Hierarchy," Blackman has shown that women held important positions in the worship of Egyptian deities. Of special interest is the *mrt,* a word referring to groups of musician-priestesses, whose function was to "rattle the sistrum" in cultic situations.[86] The evidence, as interpreted by Blackman, suggests that the *mrt* was, in some cases, the high priestess who beat the timbrel and at the same time danced and sang as the king entered the temple. Apparently by performing these rituals, the musician-priestess aimed to keep at a distance whatever was evil or distasteful to the deities as the king burned incense and offered sacrifice.

Blackman's study does not offer evidence to suggest that the timbrel

---

[85]Mowinckel (*Psalms,* 1. 22): "It appears to be a universal law that the words in the cult have taken on a rhythmic form. In rhythmic poetic form the 'force' of the words is more obvious both to perception and to emotion, and is further heightened by the music."

[86]A. Blackman, "On the Position of Women in the Ancient Egyptian Hierarchy," *JEA* 7 (1921) 8-30, esp. pp. 8-9. The musician-priestess is also referred to by the words ḥnywt and šmꜥywt. The likeness of the word *mrt* to the beginning of Miriam's name, as well as the similarity between their characteristic ritual function and the action attributed to Miriam in Exod 15:20-21 make it tempting to see in this Egyptian word a connection with Miriam's name. However, since Miriam's name does not have the final t of the Egyptian priestesses, it appears best to stay with the conclusions about the etymology of Miriam's name as discussed at the end of chap. 1.

was in a special way connected with victory celebrations. However, if the "rattling of the sistrum" in ancient Egypt was a ritual intended to drive away evil and hence to call down blessing upon the worshippers, it seems reasonable to suggest that there is an analogy in Miriam's cultic use of the timbrel. If this is the case, Miriam's playing of the timbrel, like her dance and song, must not be viewed as an empty or arbitrarily chosen joy-filled gesture, but as ritual used to accompany the life-creating and life-sustaining action of the Divine Warrior as the Divinity became present again in the symbolic re-presentation of saving deeds on Israel's behalf.

CONCLUSIONS

The similarity of Miriam's activity with that of Jephthah's daughter (Judg 11:34) and the women who greeted Saul and David (1 Sam 18:6) clearly indicates that Miriam's celebration was a victory celebration. Unlike Judg 11:34 and 1 Sam 18:6, however, the victory celebration which Miriam led was specifically cultic in nature. The hymnic character of the song in Exod 15:21 has long been recognized. But what has gone unnoticed in previous studies is the cultic character of Miriam's dance, that as ritual action the dance and song were intended as cultic re-presentations of the victory of the Divine Warrior, and possible analogies between Miriam's use of the timbrel and ancient Near Eastern witnesses to the cultic use of this instrument. This study shows, then, that Exod 15:20-21 is cultic through and through.

Because the victory celebration which Miriam led honored the Divine Warrior and not a human one, and because her activities described in Exod 15:20-21 can clearly be seen as ritual actions proper, I must disagree with those who hold that the *Sitz im Leben* for this text is to be found in the ancient Near Eastern custom of women going out to greet victorious warriors.[87] Rather, the thoroughly cultic character of Miriam's celebration and its similarities to other celebrations of Israel's Divine Warrior support the likelihood that the original *Sitz im Leben* for this text was not

---

[87]E.g., Noth, *Exodus*, 122. H. W. F. Saggs (*The Greatness That Was Babylon* [London: Sidgwick & Jackson, 1962] 190) doubts that any example of dance in the Hebrew scriptures can properly be regarded as "secular" custom: "Dancing . . . is so intimately related to the cult that it is perhaps not fitting to put it down as a pastime, as it may not yet in any sense have partaken of the nature of an independent activity." Cf. E. L. Backman, *Religious Dances* (London: George Allen and Unwin, 1952) 1, and van der Leeuw, *Religion in Essence and Manifestation*, 375.

a spontaneous celebration (e.g., like that of Jephthah's daughter) but a liturgical event at the Hebrew shrine. The celebration which Exod 15:20-21 describes would have been most appropriate during the period of the wilderness wanderings. At some later time (e.g., during the Conquest) such a celebration of Israel's Divine Warrior was probably adapted to include an expanded motif of Yahweh's victories, and, under the influence of royal theology, the expanded motif became a secondary element in the celebration of Yahweh's kingship.

What does this text say about the biblical portrait of Miriam?

First of all, many scholars view Exod 15:20-21 as belonging to the earliest stratum of Israel's literary tradition. If this view is correct, Miriam was very much alive in the memories of the earliest generations of Hebrew writers. Moreover, the fact that she is linked with nothing less than the foundational event of Hebrew religion would seem to indicate that she was viewed as having been quite a prominent person in Israel's pre-Conquest community.

Secondly, in this, her initial appearance in the texts, Miriam is portrayed as an authentic leader in the community. It is striking that according to the earliest writers she, not Moses, leads the cultic celebration of the Sea event. She appears as a leader without introduction and, as it were, without credentials. Readers are given no account of her rise to such a position. This suggests that although this is her first appearance in the texts, it was not the beginning of a "Miriam tradition." At one time there must have been a fuller account of her place in Hebrew life than what appears in the seven texts which mention her.

Finally, my study of this text shows that Miriam was remembered as a *religious* leader in Israel's early community. Moreover it firmly attests that the arena for her activity was specifically the cult. She is portrayed as the one who first articulated the religious dimension of the escape from the Egyptians at the sea. Her song, dance and playing of the timbrel were not arbitrarily chosen joyful expressions belonging to secular life. Rather, like all ritual action, they were intended as symbolically representing the saving act being celebrated.

3

Miriam: Prophetess?

In the preceding chapter it was shown that the portrait of Miriam reflected in the early tradition of Exod 15:20-21 was that of a leader and that the sphere for her activity as a leader was specifically the cult of Israel. In that chapter the designations of Miriam as prophetess and as Aaron's sister which appear in Exod 15:20 were set aside. In this chapter and in the one which follows, these two designations shall be treated with a view to recovering what light they shed on the biblical portrait of Miriam.

The present chapter focuses on the biblical witness that Miriam was a prophetess. In secondary studies the prophetess designation is sometimes used to characterize Miriam's role in Israelite tradition. Scholars cite the title which appears in Exod 15:20 and then frequently use it as a basis for understanding Miriam's role in the difficult narrative of Num 12:1-15. These two texts, therefore, are the focus for study here.

My examination of these texts will include several steps. I shall begin by offering a brief survey of those texts in which prophetesses (besides Miriam) appear in order to clarify what Hebrew writers intended by this title. Then I must ask whether or not Miriam fits the role of prophetess. I shall attempt to show that the texts never attribute true prophetic activity to Miriam. The title in Exod 15:20 has the appearance of being anachronistic. As such, it should not be used as a basis for characterizing Miriam's role in Numbers 12.

I shall also consider the portrait of Miriam in Numbers 12. A superficial reading of that text shows that the writer intended primarily to make a statement about the place of Moses (not Miriam) in Israelite tradition. Therefore, in order to know what the text says about Miriam, it will be necessary first of all to clarify what the Hebrew writer was saying about Moses. I shall suggest that the divine proclamation of vv 6-8 was an originally independent tradition which aimed at clarifying Moses' position vis-à-vis prophets. Moses here appears to be a figure representing the oracular authority claimed by the Levites. A later writer used the early (pre-Deuteronomic) divine declaration of Num 12:6-8 to settle a struggle for oracular authority between an Aaronic group of priests (represented by Aaron and Miriam) and the Levites (represented by Moses). In the controversy of Num 12:2-9, then, Miriam is portrayed as voicing the ✓ concerns of a priestly, not a prophetic group.

Finally, it will be seen that the controversy of Num 12:2-9 has been inserted into an early story of Miriam's controversy with Moses over his Cushite wife (v 1) and her resulting punishment by leprosy (vv 10ff.). The writers attempted to harmonize the earlier tradition of vv 1, 10ff. with the later tradition of vv 2-9 by introducing Aaron into the former.

As a context for studying the designation of Miriam as prophetess, a brief survey of the place of prophetesses in Hebrew religion is offered here.

PROPHETESSES IN ISRAEL

A survey of the texts which speak of prophetesses in Israel shows that they belong to nearly every stage of Hebrew biblical tradition and that the designation of "prophetess" implied the same gifts and functions as the term "prophet."

According to Judg 4:6f. the prophetess Deborah announced to Barak Yahweh's intention to release the Israelites from Canaanite oppression and later (4:14f.) it was her cry which signalled the engagement of battle. The two oracles attributed to Deborah have much in common with the oracles of other prophets: (1) The oracle of Judg 4:6f. consists of a proclamation of what the troops are to do and what the Lord is doing. Deborah's statement of what the Lord is doing (4:7) is issued in the first person indicating that the words which are being spoken belong not to Deborah but to Yahweh.[1] (2) The words "I will give him [i.e., the enemy]

---

[1] According to the RSV translation the oracle of Judg 4:6 is introduced with the following words: "The Lord, the God of Israel, commands you . . ." It should be noted, however, that in the Hebrew text, the words begin with an interrogative particle. A more accurate translation is the rhetorical "Has not the Lord . . . commanded you . . .?" It is difficult to know whether this construction was intended to be comparable to the recurrent phrase, "Thus says the Lord," used by the classical prophets and also by pre-classical prophets in oracles concerning war (e.g., 1 Sam 15:2, 1 Kgs 12:24, 1 Kgs 22:11, 1 Kgs 20:13, 28). On the use of the introductory for-

into your hand," are characteristic of an expression used by other prophets before battle (cf. 1 Kgs 22:6, 12, 15; 1 Kgs 20:13, 28). (3) In Deborah's oracle of v 14, the use of the perfect tense ("The Lord has given Sisera into your hand") reflects a characteristic of other prophetic oracles, i.e., that the pronouncement of the oracular figure exercised a decisive influence on what was to come. When the oracle was delivered, its message was as good as accomplished. (4) Finally, the fact that Deborah's oracles concerned the entire community and Yahweh's intention with regard to their inheritance of the land indicates that a prophetess, like prophets, could be and in fact were duly authorized to articulate matters of national and sacral concern to the whole body of the people.

Little can be said with certainty of the unnamed prophetess of Isa 8:3. No distinctive prophetic activity is attributed to her. The text simply says that she was the mother of Isaiah's son. Consequently, most scholars regard her simply as the prophet's wife.[2] Some have suggested that it was customary for the wife of a prophet to be called a prophetess.[3] However, there is no other indication that an Israelite woman received a title which derived from her husband's profession.[4] Even if this could be proven, it need not follow that the explanation of the prophetess in Isa 8:3 has been fully exhausted. Several other possibilities have been advanced: (1) that she was a prophetess in her own right;[5] (2) that the conception of Isaiah's son was regarded as a prophetic sign and that the boy's mother was a prophetess insofar as she was the "bearer of the powerful word of the

---

mula and on the word of the prophet(ess) as the word of God, see C. Westermann, *Basic Forms of Prophetic Speech* (Philadelphia: Westminster, 1967), especially pp. 90-128. Cf. a recent critique of Westermann's view of the prophet as God's messenger in G. M. Tucker, "Prophetic Speech," *Int* 32 (1978) 31-45.

[2]Cf. H. G. May, "An Interpretation of the Names of Hosea's Children," *JBL* 55 (1936) 285-91, who has advanced the possibility that she was a sacred prostitute.

[3]See, e.g., Haldar, *Associations of Cult Prophets*, 109, n. 1; E. J. Young, *The Book of Isaiah*, NICOT (Grand Rapids, MI: Wm. B. Eerdmanns, 1965) 303; cf. R. B. Y. Scott, "The Book of Isaiah," in *IB* (1956) 5. 223, and especially I. W. Slotki, *Isaiah*, Soncino Books of the Bible (London: Soncino, 1949) 38: "A husband confers his title upon his wife irrespective of her own qualifications and attainments."

[4]Vos, *Woman in Old Testament Worship*, 187.

[5]J. Lindblom, *Prophecy in Ancient Israel* (Philadelphia: Muhlenberg, 1962) 169.

Lord;"[6] (3) that she was identified with the ʿalmâh of Isaiah 7 and that ʿalmâh is a term which in certain contexts, referred to female temple musicians with ecstatic gifts.[7] Since the text offers no information on the prophetic activity of the woman of Isa 8:3, these interpretations must all remain at the level of conjecture. The mention of the prophetess in this case, then, sheds little light on the role of prophetesses in Israel.

Although not much is known of the prophetess Huldah, she appears to have held a position of great importance in Jerusalem during the latter part of the seventh century B.C. When King Josiah learned that a book of the law had been found during the repair of the Temple, he directed his officials to "inquire of the Lord" for him, for the people, and for all Judah concerning the book. 2 Kgs 22:14-15 reports:

> So Hilkiah, the priest, and Ahikam, and Achbor, and Shaphan, and Asaiah went to Huldah the prophetess, the wife of Shallum . . . keeper of the wardrobe (now she dwelt in the Second Quarter); and they talked with her. And she said to them: "Thus says the Lord . . ."

Since the final decision to undertake the Josianic reform is represented as resting upon Huldah's judgment, one can assume that she held some official capacity in Jerusalem at the time.[8] If the reform was largely a matter of legitimate cultic practice and if the reform stemmed from the

---

[6]A. S. Herbert, *The Book of the Prophet Isaiah: Chapters I-XXXIX,* The Cambridge Bible Commentary (Cambridge: Cambridge University, 1973) 67.

[7]N. K. Gottwald, "Immanuel as the Prophet's Son," *VT* 8 (1958) 36-47 (see esp., 44-45). Cf. H. M. Wolf, "A Solution to the Immanuel Prophecy in Isaiah 7:14-8:22," *JBL* 91 (1972) 449-56.

[8]Several commentators have attempted to deal with the fact that Huldah and not her contemporary, the prophet Jeremiah, was consulted over such an important concern. Some (see the survey of opinions in Vos, *Woman in Old Testament Worship,* 184-85) have suggested that Jeremiah had not yet received widespread recognition while others are of the opinion that he was known but unpopular in Jerusalem circles. J. Gray's suggestion (*I and II Kings,* 2nd ed., OTL [Philadelphia: Westminster, 1970] 726) that Huldah, being the wife of a Temple official, was regarded as more likely to render the approval which priests sought and thus less likely than Jeremiah to upset the status quo, has no foundation in the text.

recovered book, it is probable that Huldah's position was in some way connected with the official cult.[9]

Huldah's use of the common prophetic formula, "thus says the Lord," indicates that her judgment was regarded as the word of the Lord.[10] This impression is reinforced by Josiah's directive, "Go, inquire of the Lord." Her activity, then, resembles that of Deborah in Judges 4-5. Like Deborah, she speaks on behalf of the welfare of the entire community.

Although the texts yield little specific information about prophetesses in later periods of Hebrew history, it seems certain that they continued to be active in religious circles. Ezek 13:17-23 indicates realistically that female as well as male prophets were capable of leading the people astray. In Neh 6:14 the prophetess Noadiah is named along with other officials as an adversary of Nehemiah's reconstruction efforts in Jerusalem.[11] Finally Joel 3:1 counts prophetesses as well as prophets among the blessings of the Age to Come. While these texts, like Isa 8:3, witness to the existence of prophetesses in Israel, they do not offer specific information regarding the activity and position of prophetic women in Israel.

This admittedly brief and incomplete survey of prophetesses in the

---

[9]N. H. Snaith (*IB* [1954] 3. 318) views Huldah as a cultic prophetess attached to the Jerusalem Temple. J. Gray (*I and II Kings*, 726-27) says that the "Second Quarter" of Jerusalem might have been a residential area for palace and Temple personnel. It is noteworthy that Huldah is described as the wife of a Temple official although this, of course, need not imply that she too was one. Cf. Lindblom (*Prophecy in Ancient Israel*, 210), who regards Huldah as an independent prophetess and not part of the Temple staff.

[10]See references cited in n. 1 above.

[11]Lindblom (*Prophecy in Ancient Israel*, 218) has suggested that all those referred to in Neh 6:10-14 were Temple prophets. The textual witness on the designation of Noadiah as prophetess is interesting. Most versions render the designation as masculine, i.e., "prophet." The translators may have identified the Noadiah of Neh 6:14 with that of Ezra 8:33, a (male) Levite with some official status at the Temple in Jerusalem, although this explanation seems unlikely in view of the fact that the text offers no indication that the Noadiah of Ezra 8 held a prophetic position or that he was in opposition to the work of Ezra. On the other hand, the variants may reflect a hesitancy to portray a prophetess as having some official status during this period. It is also noteworthy that the "rest of the prophets" mentioned in connection with Noadiah in Neh 6:14 is translated "the rest of the priests" by several versions. See R. A. Bowman, *IB* (1954) 3. 721.

Hebrew scriptures shows that the narratives make no effort to explain the phenomenon of prophetesses or to indicate that the appearance of prophetesses was regarded in any way as exceptional. This, plus the textual representation of the activity of Deborah and Huldah, suggests that the content of the "prophetess" designation was meant to include the same content as the designation "prophet."[12] Hence, prophetesses, like prophets, were regarded as mediators of the Lord's word and, as such, they were oracular authorities in sacral matters which might pertain to the entire community.

With this in mind, I now turn to the two texts which, according to modern scholarship, reflect Miriam's prophetic role.

EXODUS 15:20-21

Exod 15:20 is the only text in the scriptures which specifically designates Miriam as a prophetess. Some have understood the juxtaposition of Miriam's dance and song and the designation of her as prophetess as indicative that she was an ecstatic.[13] It is true that music and dance were means used by ancient Near Eastern and early Hebrew prophets presumably for the purpose of evoking ecstasy.[14] Furthermore, Haldar cites an example from ancient Near Eastern practice in which ritual combat appears to be linked with ecstatic dance.[15] Thus, while there are grounds for suggesting that Miriam was an ecstatic prophetess, one must proceed cautiously. If ecstatic prophecy is taken to mean a condition in which

---

[12]A notable exception, of course, is that no prophetesses belong to the phenomenon called classical prophecy in Israel. General works on prophets in Israel include B. W. Anderson and W. Harrelson, eds., *Israel's Prophetic Heritage: Essays in Honor of James Muilenberg* (New York: Harper and Row, 1962); A. J. Heschel, *The Prophets* (2 vols.; New York: Harper and Row, 1963); A. R. Johnson, *The Cultic Prophet in Ancient Israel*, 2nd ed. (Cardiff: University of Wales, 1962); Lindblom, *Prophecy in Ancient Israel*; G. von Rad, *Old Testament Theology* (2 vols.; New York: Harper and Row, 1965). In addition, see the entire January, 1978 issue of *Int* 32.

[13]Noth, *Exodus*, 123; Hyatt, *A Commentary on Exodus*, 169; R. E. Clements, *Exodus*, The Cambridge Bible Commentary (Cambridge: Cambridge University, 1972) 93; J. C. Rylaarsdam, "The Book of Exodus," in *IB* (1952) 1. 945.

[14]See, e.g., Lindblom, *Prophecy in Ancient Israel*, 59-60.

[15]Haldar, *Associations of Cult Prophets*, 58.

ordinary processes of human consciousness are temporarily suspended[16] as, for example in 1 Sam 19:20ff., then it is difficult to see in Exod 15:20f. sufficient evidence for regarding Miriam as an ecstatic. Also, one must question whether Miriam's celebration can be compared to the frenzy of the ecstatic prophets of 1 Sam 10:5ff. and 1 Kgs 18:26ff. In the preceding chapter it was shown that Miriam's dance and song bear close resemblance to the rituals of other Hebrew victory celebrations and there is little evidence which suggests that these rituals as employed in victory celebrations generally bore an ecstatic character.[17] One must conclude, then, that the information given in Exod 15:20f. is too slight to firmly link Miriam's activity as described there with ecstatic prophecy.

When compared with those characteristics outlined above (pp. 42-43), one can see that Miriam's celebration of the Divine Warrior bears little relationship to the actions of other prophetic figures connected with war. The song of Exod 15:21 bears the formal characteristics of a hymn and not those of an oracle. Miriam leads the community in a proclamation of faith and this, of course, differs significantly from delivering the Lord's word to the community. She does not speak regarding the outcome of a forthcoming battle but rather articulates the religious dimension of a past victory. Since there appears to have been no human element involved in the Hebrews' successful escape from the Egyptians at the sea, Miriam could not be portrayed as a military (prophetic) advisor. Of other prophetic figures connected with war, Miriam bears closest resemblance to Deborah but that is so only because leadership in victory hymns is attributed to both.

What, then, is the content of the title which appears in Exod 15:20? Many scholars agree that the designation of Miriam as prophetess is an anachronism (similar to the designations of Abraham, Aaron and Moses as prophets), i.e., the result of later religious personnel wishing to claim predecessors in the earliest stages of Hebrew religion.[18] The probability of this suggestion is strengthened in cases like Exod 15:20f. where the tradition did not record any specific prophetic activity in connection with the person called a prophet or prophetess. The probability that the

---

[16]Lindblom, *Prophecy in Ancient Israel*, 106; Haldar, *Associations of Cult Prophets*, 21ff.

[17]A possible exception is David's wild dance before the Ark in 2 Samuel 6.

[18]Lindblom, *Prophecy in Ancient Israel*, 96, n. 71, 99-100; von Rad, *Old Testament Theology*, 2. 12; C. Kuhl, *The Prophets of Israel* (Richmond, VA: John Knox, 1960) 9.

designation is an anachronism is further strengthened in the case of Miriam for the following reason: since all seven of the scriptural texts which mention Miriam link her firmly with the pre-Conquest period, one is safe in assuming that she indeed did belong to that period. The traditions about Miriam to which later writers were heir presented her as an important religious functionary at this early stage of Hebrew religion. However, the fragmentary nature of the literary traditions about Miriam suggests that these later writers did not have access to a complete account of Miriam's role in the community. A later writer, considering it advisable to further identify Miriam, might well have been forced to turn to religious functionaries of his own day for a role by which to designate Miriam's position. Since prophetesses appear to have been common in Israelite circles, the prophetic designation would have been readily available.

While Exod 15:20, then, says that Miriam was a prophetess, one must be cautious in attributing to her the roles and functions of later Israelite prophets and prophetesses. Considering the absence of an account of any true prophetic activity on her part and the likelihood that the designation is simply an anachronism, it seems best to conclude that the prophetess designation in Exod 15:20 adds little to the overall portrait of Miriam in the bible.

Why was the designation included in the text about the celebration of Israel's Divine Warrior? The answer probably lies in the fact that Miriam had not yet been introduced in the texts. Some writer no doubt felt it advantageous to further identify her before recounting her activity in the community. It seems to be the Elohist strand which frequently (and anachronistically) attests to a prophetic element in the earliest stages of Israelite religion. Therefore the prophetess designation in Exod 15:20 might tentatively be regarded as the Elohist's contribution to that text.

NUMBERS 12

Num 12:1-15 is the longest text about Miriam in the scriptures. Unfortunately the text is also very complex. Since the present chapter is primarily concerned with the biblical witness that Miriam was a prophetess, and since vv 2-9 is the only section of Numbers 12 which portrays Miriam as an oracular figure, I shall begin with a treatment of those verses. However, vv 2-9 are closely bound to the surrounding narrative of Num 12:1-15. Therefore, this chapter will be extended to include an analysis of vv 1, 10ff. as well.

In view of the sparse treatment which Numbers 12 has received in scholarly literature,[19] one is not surprised that the subject of Miriam's role in this narrative has been given only passing reference. When she is discussed, scholars have generally interpreted Miriam's role in Numbers 12 in light of the prophetess designation of Exod 15:20. A few examples will suffice. In an attempt to explain the divine proclamation of vv 6-8 and the fact that it is addressed to Miriam and Aaron, Noth writes:

> In Miriam's case reference is certainly . . . made to the designation of her by tradition as a "prophetess" (Ex. 15:20). Aaron, on the other hand, is not otherwise known to tradition as a recipient of the word independently of Moses. Was he perhaps placed as the male partner of Miriam in the present context only because that seemed desirable in this case and because, as a well-known figure in Moses' sphere of activity, he was specially suited to such a role?[20]

---

[19]To my knowledge, the problematic narrative of Num 12:1-15 has not been singled out for detailed study. For the most part, the passage has been treated in studies which deal with controversy stories in the wilderness narratives. G. W. Coats (*Rebellion in the Wilderness: The Murmuring Motif in the Wilderness Traditions of the Old Testament* [Nashville: Abingdon, 1968]) does not regard Numbers 12 as belonging to the murmuring motif and consequently treats it briefly in an appendix to his work. V. Fritz (*Israel in der Wüste* [Marburg: N. G. Elwert, 1970]) has a brief analysis which he devotes almost exclusively to the story of Miriam's leprosy (Num 12:1, 9a, 10ab, 13-15). A. Tunyogi (*The Rebellions of Israel* [Richmond: John Knox, 1969]) gives Numbers 12 even briefer treatment, as do similar studies on the theology and/or sociology and/or anthropology which stands behind the murmuring traditions (see, e.g., R. P. Carroll, "Rebellion and Dissent in Ancient Israelite Society," *ZAW* 89 [1977] 176-204; S. J. de Vries, "The Origin of the Murmuring Tradition," *JBL* 87 [1968] 51-58; J. A. Wilcoxen, "Some Anthropocentric Aspects of Israel's Sacred History," *JR* 48 [1968] 333-50. Num 12:6-8 has been treated separately in connection with the biblical motif of Moses' uniqueness. See the references to this literature within the analysis of these verses. Also to be noted is the cursory treatment of Num 12:1-16 in the section on "intervention as punishment" in R. C. Culley's *Studies in the Structure of Hebrew Narrative* (Missoula, Montana: Scholar's, 1976) 104-6. The very general nature of Culley's treatment of Numbers 12, however, renders it particularly unhelpful for the present study.

[20]*Numbers*, 93.

Coats[21] views Miriam as a prophetic prototype in the controversy of Num 12:2-9 and, in so doing, he (like Noth) cites the Exod 15:20 tradition. He goes on to suggest that vv 2-9 stem from a conflict between Aaronic and Levitical priests but does not address himself to the question of the place of Miriam as prophetic prototype within that conflict. Tunyogi[22] mentions Numbers 12 only briefly but views it as belonging to a group of rebellions in which only cultic personnel participated. (He does not substantiate that Miriam belonged to cultic personnel.) The controversy of Num 12:2ff., according to Tunyogi, was intended to assert Moses' uniqueness as Yahweh's representative and, as such, he says that the story reflects a prophetic—not a priestly—conflict.[23] Since this hardly explains the place of Aaron in the controversy, Tunyogi suggests that the entire narrative is a rebellion of Miriam against the absoluteness of Moses' position and he regards the mention of Aaron as a secondary insertion into the controversy. Tunyogi, like Noth and Coats, bases his interpretation of Miriam as prophetess in Numbers 12 on the Exod 15:20 designation.

As a response to these views, let me simply point out that my study of the designation of Miriam as prophetess in Exod 15:20 shows that this text is hardly a firm foundation upon which to understand Miriam's role in Numbers 12. The title in Exod 15:20 has the appearance of being anachronistic. While the prophetess title bears some general affinity to the portrait of Miriam as an oracular figure in Numbers 12, there is no explicit connection between the two texts and to interpret one in terms of the other is overstepping the biblical evidence. Miriam's role in Numbers 12, then, must be understood apart from Exod 15:20. A proper understanding of her role in Numbers 12 must arise from that text alone.

A superficial reading of Num 12:2-9 shows that the focal point of that narrative is not Miriam but Moses. In order to understand Miriam's role there it is necessary first to examine what the text says about Moses. A preliminary treatment of Moses' role (vv 6-8) shall prepare for a study of the larger context (vv 2-9) and Miriam's role in it.

---

[21]Coats, *Rebellion in the Wilderness*, 261-4.

[22]Tunyogi, *The Rebellions of Israel*, 48.

[23]R. R. Wilson, ("Early Israelite Prophecy," in *Int* 32 [1978] 12) also views Numbers 12 as a prophetic controversy. Cf. Noth, *Pentateuchal Traditions*, 128-9.

NUMBERS 12:6-8
MOSES AND THE PROPHETS

Num 12:2-9 relates a controversy brought forth by Aaron and Miriam regarding Moses' singular oracular authority. The narrative follows the lines of a quickly executed drama: the conflict is abruptly initiated (v 2); the transition to the Tent (vv 4-5); the defense states its case (vv 6-8); and the conflict is abruptly resolved (v 9). The climax of the dramatic action appears in the proclamation of vv 6-8:

(v 6)   Hear my words:
If there is a prophet among you,[24]
I the Lord make myself known to him in a vision,
I speak with him in a dream.

(v 7)   Not so with my servant Moses;
he is entrusted with all my house.

---

[24]The MT of v 6b is hopelessly difficult. If translated literally the line might be read: "If Yahweh is your prophet . . ." If read with the rest of the verse this translation is difficult to understand. Hence, various alternatives have been proposed: BHK follows the major versions (LXX, Vg, Sam. Tg.) in reading "Yahweh" with the introductory verb in the verse, "and Yahweh said" (the variants then add the indirect object, "to them"). The OL and Vg read *nâbî bâkem* ("prophet among you") instead of *nĕbî'ăkem* ("your prophet") and prefix *lamed* to *yhwh*: "If there is a prophet of Yahweh among you . . ." The LXX does not alter the *nĕbî'ăkem* ("your prophet") of the MT but does add the *lamed* to *yhwh*: "If your prophet belong to Yahweh . . ." Modern translators generally render the same sense as the RSV. See G. B. Gray, *A Critical and Exegetical Commentary on Numbers*, ICC (New York: Charles Scribner's Son, 1906) 124-5; Albright, *Yahweh and the Gods of Canaan* (London: Athlone, 1968) 37; Cross, *Canaanite Myth and Hebrew Epic*, 203; J. S. Kselman, "A Note on Nm. XII:6-8," *VT* 26 (1976) 500ff.; Freedman, "The Aaronic Benediction (Numbers 6:24-26)," in *No Famine in the Land: Studies in Honor of John L. McKenzie*, ed. J. M. Flanagan and A. W. Robinson (Missoula, Montana: Scholar's, 1975), 42ff.; Noth, *Numbers*, 92; N. H. Snaith, *Leviticus and Numbers*, The Century Bible (London: Thomas Nelson and Sons, 1967) 235; cf. A. R. Johnson, *The Cultic Prophet in Ancient Israel* 46-7, n. 7.

(v 8)   With him I speak mouth to mouth,[25]
           clearly and not in dark speech;
           and he beholds the form of the Lord.[26]

           Why then were you not afraid to speak against my
           servant Moses?

There is reason to regard Num 12:6-8 as a unit which was originally
independent of Num 12:2-9. Noth points out that the Divinity's words are
"in an elevated style, yet without being rhythmically constructed."[27]
More detailed studies of recent years have attempted to delineate the
poetic structure of the passage. In a proposed reconstruction, Cross[28]
views Num 12:6-8 as a poem consisting of a tricolon (v 6), a bicolon (v 7),
and a concluding tricolon (v 8), with all but one line (v 7a) seven syllables
in length. Using Cross's reconstruction, Kselman[29] points out the literary
characteristics of repetition, assonance, and word play which suggest an
ABCD-D'C'B'A' structure to the poem. Freedman, too, finds a poetic
structure in vv 6-8.[30] He shows a poem consisting of an initial unit of two

---

[25]A slight variation of this expression occurs in Jer 32:4 and 34:3
where the MT says that Zedekiah will meet the king of Babylon and speak
with him "mouth to mouth" (cf. the RSV translation "face to face") and
see him "eye to eye." (Cf. 2 Kgs 10:21, 21:16; Ezra 9:11, where the
expression "mouth to mouth" is used as a spatial reference.) Hence, in
saying that Yahweh speaks with Moses "mouth to mouth," the author of
Numbers 12 simply asserts the directness of Moses' exchanges with the
Divinity. It is difficult to explain the departure from the synonymous
expression "face to face," which is used in Exod 33:11 and Deut 34:10.
[26]Cf. Ps 17:15 where a similar expression is used in parallel to
beholding the divine face. One must understand this as simply another
metaphorical expression which asserts Moses' direct contact with the
Divinity. Given the prohibition of těmūnâh, however, in Exod 20:4, Deut
5:8 and especially Deut 4:12, 15, 16, 23, 25, its use here is striking. The
LXX, Sam. Tg. and Tg. Onq. say that Moses beholds the "glory" of Yahweh
(cf. Exod 33:17-23).
[27]Numbers, 95.
[28]Canaanite Myth, 203-4.
[29]"A Note on Nm. XII:6-8," 500-505.
[30]Freedman, "The Aaronic Benediction" in No Famine in the Land.
Freedman's analysis differs significantly from those of Cross and
Kselman. First of all, he is much more conservative than Cross in propos-
ing textual emendations and, for the most part, adheres strictly to the

bicola (v 6), and a second unit of two bicola (v 7 and v 8d) which serves as
an envelope for a third and central unit (v 8abc), a tricolon in which the
author expresses his main point with regard to Moses' unique status.[31]

In my opinion, a recovery of the original poetic structure of this piece
is not possible, as is suggested by these conflicting analyses. Any metrical
analysis will depend on which textual witnesses are accepted,[32] not to
mention textual emendations such as Cross and Kselman have proposed.[33]
It seems preferable to simply point out literary characteristics which set
these verses apart from the surrounding narrative: (1) the "elevated style"
of vv 6-8 stands in marked contrast to the prosaic style of the surrounding
narrative; (2) the introductory formula, "Hear my words," at the beginning
of v 6 functions in such a way as to set off the lines which follow as an
official proclamation; (3) the proclamation itself is a definition of the
position of Moses vis-à-vis the position of "prophet." The distinction is set
forth in a symmetrical arrangement: (a) *dbr bĕ* is used with reference to
the prophet in v 6 and with reference to Moses in v 8 and (b) the Hebrew
mr'h is used in v 6 with reference to the mode of the Divinity's self-
revelation to the prophet and in v 8 with reference to the mode of the
Divinity's self-revelation to Moses. The Massoretes distinguished the two

---

MT. In addition, he includes the introductory words of v 6a and the closing
line of v 8 in the poetic structure.

[31] Albright, Freedman and Kselman find characteristics of Canaanite
and early Hebrew poetry in Num 12:6-8 and thus argue for a very early
dating for the piece. Noth (*Pentateuchal Traditions*, 127), on the other
hand, points out that this text presupposes a rather sophisticated reflection on the nature of "prophet" and the establishment of a certain hierarchy with regard to modes of revelation. Thus he suggests a slightly later
date (secondary addition to J). However, he correctly warns against dating
this text too late since the text offers no hint that Moses and Aaron and
Miriam were considered brothers and sister at this point (cf. Exod 6:20;
15:20; 1 Chr 5:29; Num 26:59; see *Numbers*, 94).

[32] Besides the important variants to the MT of v 6b, there are other
variants in the early versions (see Kittel's textual apparatus) which,
although they do not bear significant alterations in the sense conveyed by
the MT, would have direct bearing on the metrical structure.

[33] In my opinion, the MT and/or its major variants must always be
accepted in the absence of strong evidence to the contrary. The consequences of this position might be that some texts will forever remain
mysteries to scholars. However, this seems preferable to risking the
dangers of exegetical expedience. For a similar view, see Freedman, "The
Aaronic Benediction," 35-6.

by pointing the first *marʾâh* and the second *marʾeh*. According to the RSV translation, the distinction is that Yahweh is made known to the prophet in a "vision," but speaks "clearly" with Moses, i.e., "not in dark speech;"[34] (4) verse 8d shows a change in style and content from the lines which precede it: (a) the longer prosaic sentence stands in contrast to the compact lines of the definition of the two roles in v 6bcd and v 8abc and (b) the content is an accusation of impropriety which is based on, but not part of, the preceding definition of roles. Therefore v 8d does not appear to belong to the unit which begins in v 6.

The style and content of vv 6-8c suggests that it should be viewed as a separate unit within Num 12:2-9. Moreover, there is reason to believe that the declaration of vv 6-8c at one time circulated independently. First of all, there is nothing in the declaration which necessarily indicates that Moses' position was being questioned. Secondly, it is noteworthy that the recipients of the official proclamation are anonymous. The line, "If there is a prophet among you," might well have been addressed to any individual or group. Finally, it seems unlikely that a major declaration regarding the stance of Moses vis-à-vis prophets would have been addressed to two persons who were not characterized by the traditions as major prophetic figures in the wilderness. The point might have been made more effectively by placing the spirit-filled elders of Numbers 11 as the antagonists of Numbers 12.

Verses 6-8c do not negate the authority of those who prophesy from dreams and visions.[35] Rather, it distinguishes it from and subordinates it to Moses' gift. The rationale for the distinction lies in Moses' direct access to the divine word whereas prophets receive the word through means which need interpretation.

---

[34]Cf. Freedman, "The Aaronic Benediction," 43 and Kselman, "A Note on Nm. XII:6-8," 501. A. R. Johnson (*The Cultic Prophet in Ancient Israel* 48-9) suggests that this line (v 8b) is a reaction to the practice of "traffic in oracles," i.e., since the oracles of typical prophets were enigmatic in character and preserved in some way, they lent themselves to subsequent use by other prophets in different situations. Hence, prophets could rightly be accused of stealing oracles from one another and, in so doing, speaking out of their own thoughts. The transposed oracle, then, bore no divine authority. See, e.g., Jer 23:16.

[35]In Jeremiah 23 the same contrasts (prophecy from dreams and visions vs. prophecy by direct revelation) are used. There is a difference, however, from Numbers 12 in that Jeremiah equates prophecy from dreams and visions with false prophecy (cf. Jer 27:9; 29:8; Deut 13:4, etc.)

The view that Moses had unique access to the divine word is a recurring
motif in the Pentateuchal traditions. For the most part his direct
encounters with the Divinity were connected with Sinai and with the Tent
of Meeting[36] and the encounters at these places were unequivocally
connected with Moses' role as mediator of Yahweh's word. Hence, in the
Sinai narratives Moses ascended the mountain not to see but to converse
with God. When he returned to the community he announced the Lord's
will in the form of the covenantal laws. Likewise, Exod 33:7-11 does not
say that Moses saw Yahweh at the Tent of Meeting but rather that Yahweh spoke "face to face" (i.e., directly) with Moses there.

Other texts are even more explicit in linking Moses' direct encounters
with Yahweh with his role as mediator of the divine covenantal word.
According to Exod 20:19ff., the peoples' fear of direct encounter with the
Divinity at Sinai led them to petition Moses to act as intermediary.[37]

> You speak to us, and we will hear;
> but let not God speak to us lest we die.

In another account of the same event, Deut 5:4 says that Yahweh spoke
"face to face" with the people at the mountain although the following
verse emends that by having Moses remind the people that he "stood
between Yahweh and you at that time, to declare to you the word of the
Lord; for you were afraid . . ." Deut 18:15ff. reflects the same tradition

----

[36]M. Haran ("From Early to Classical Prophecy: Continuity and
Change," VT 27 [1977] 386) suggests that the encounter at Sinai was
patterned after the institutionalized oracular activity associated with the
Tent of Meeting.

[37]The fear which accompanied the thought of speaking directly with
God bears direct relation to the fear of seeing God. The Pentateuchal
traditions reflect the view that it is possible for humans to see God but
that that experience is normally expected to result in the death of the
beholder. See, e.g., Gen 32:31, Exod 24:11 (cf. Judg 13:22). This even
applies to Moses (Exod 33:17-23). Note, however, Exod 24:9-11, which says
that quite a large group saw God on Sinai. Some scholars have argued that
the earliest strata of the tradition bore the understanding that the vision
of God did not have fatal consequences. See, for example, the series of
articles by E. W. Nicholson: "The Interpretation of Ex. XXIV 9-11," VT 24
(1974) 77-97; "The Antiquity of the Tradition in Ex. XXIV 9-11," VT 25
(1975) 69-79; "The Tradition in Ex. XXIV 9-11," VT 26 (1976) 148-60; and
D. N. Freedman, "The Aaronic Benediction," 35-48.

and in that context promises that in the future the Lord would raise up a "prophet like Moses" who would serve the same function.

Given this weighty portrait of Moses, one is not surprised to find a complementary tradition which says that other oracular figures in the community derive their authority from Moses. Hence, according to Exodus 18, Jethro advised Moses to choose "able men" and to "teach them the statutes and decisions" so that Moses would not be so burdened with those who sought the Lord's word.[38] The subsequent narrative makes clear that the power of appointment of Israel's judicial authorities rested with Moses (v 25) but that Moses retained supremacy in delivering decisive judgments (vv 22, 26). It should be noted that the locus for these appointments was Sinai, the place of the covenantal revelation.

The Exodus 18 "relief from the burden" motif has a parallel in Num 11:14-17, 24b-30.[39] At the Tent of Meeting "the Lord came down in a cloud and spoke to him [Moses], and took some of the spirit that was upon him and put it upon the seventy elders; and when the spirit rested on them they prophesied . . ." (v 25).[40] Insofar as the elder's spirit of prophecy

---

[38]Note that in the parallel account of Deut 1:9-18 there is no reference to the role of Jethro. Noth (Pentateuchal Traditions, 136) is of the opinion that the motif of the easing of Moses' burden was originally independent of the visit of Jethro. The two traditions were probably joined because the Hebrew word maśâ² means both "oracle" and "burden." Cf. Jer 23:23ff.

[39]It is widely recognized that the motif of the seventy elders is a later insertion into a narrative which tells of the lack of meat in the wilderness and of Yahweh's response to that need (see Coats, Rebellion in the Wilderness, 97-8 and sources cited there). Noth, Pentateuchal Traditions, 127, 129-30 and Numbers 88-90) and von Rad (Old Testament Theology, 2. 8-9) regard the motif of the elders as a legitimation of the phenomenon of ecstatic prophecy which has been reflected back into the wilderness period (cf. Lindblom, Prophecy in Ancient Israel, 100-02). Von Rad (Old Testament Theology, 2. 9) warns against dating this addition to Numbers 11 too late: ". . . it is . . . early in the sense in which it supplies evidence of an encounter with the prophetic movement and some discussion of it. It still preserves echoes of the amazement to which this strange event gave rise, and of the effort to come to some intellectual understanding of such an unprecedented phenomenon."

[40]The welō² yâsâpû ("but they did so no more") at the end of v 25 is problematic. Noth (Numbers, 89) accepts the tradition of the Tg. and Vg in translating "and they did so unceasingly" (welō² yâsūpû).

derived from Moses, the unique position of Moses as bearer of the divine word is again asserted.

Numbers 11 and Exodus 18 agree, then, that the oracular authority of others within the community receives its authenticity from the fact that it derives from Moses. This assertion is probably an extension of the tradition which regards the oracular authority of Moses as absolute and unique. In light of this, Num 11:26-30 must be examined. There Moses endorses the prophecy of Eldad and Medad even though their prophecy did not derive from him.[41] Regardless of its apparent departure from the motif of Moses' oracular uniqueness, the fact remains and is significant that the legitimacy of the prophetic circle represented by Eldad and Medad depends upon Moses' endorsement.

It is not difficult to see that Num 12:6-8c stands firmly within the tradition which viewed Moses' oracular authority as uniquely superior. Like Exod 20:19ff., 33:7-11, Deut 5:4f. and Deut 18:15ff., the rationale given for Moses' uniqueness in Numbers 12 is his direct access to the divine word. And, like Exodus 18 and Num 11:14-17, 24b-30, it asserts that, while there are others in the community who have access to the divine word, Moses bears this power in a unique sense.[42]

If Num 12:6-8, like most of the wilderness traditions, is a reflection of later religious concerns which have been projected back into the "archetypal" period of the wilderness,[43] one must ask: who is the Moses who is represented here? The answer to this question might eventually help to clarify the roles of Miriam and Aaron in the surrounding narrative.

Two possibilities come to mind. In ancient Israel two different groups of people functioned as interpreters of the Deity's word: priests and

---

[41]Noth (*Numbers*, 90) has pointed out the difficulty of this episode within the context of Num 11:14-17, 24-25. Cf. von Rad, *Old Testament Theology*, 2. 9 and Lindblom, *Prophecy in Ancient Israel*, 102.

[42]Noth (*Numbers*, 93) regards Numbers 12 as an expansion, or "even a correction" of Num 11:14-17, 24b-30. That is to say, the author of Numbers 12 wants to make clear that Moses is not just another ecstatic prophet. I would agree, however, with von Rad (*Old Testament Theology*, 2. 9-10) that one must be cautious in equating those who prophesy from the "spirit of Yahweh" (Numbers 11) with those with whom Yahweh has spoken (Numbers 12), even if that *dbr* comes through dreams and visions.

[43]On the archetypal character of the wilderness narratives, see, e.g. von Rad, *Old Testament Theology*, 1. 290; Noth, *Pentateuchal Traditions*, 127-28 and R. P. Carroll, "Rebellion and Dissent in Ancient Israelite Society."

prophets. Priestly oracles were generally connected with technical means (e.g., *urim* and *thummim*) while prophetic revelation rested largely upon contact with the Divinity through more pneumatic means (e.g., dreams, visions, and the coming of the "spirit"). As priests came to be preoccupied with increasing specialization in the sacrificial cult of the Temple, oracular activity came more and more to be connected with prophets. The Levitical priests, however, remained as oracular functionaries, employing the more technical means of discerning the Lord's word but also deriving the divine will from the covenantal word with which they had been entrusted by Moses. Prophetic oracles continued to be rooted in revelation through ecstatic experiences.[44]

Given this background, I return to the question: whom does the Moses of Num 12:6-8 represent? The most obvious possibility, perhaps, is that behind the figure of Moses stands one (cultic?) prophet whose superiority over other prophets is based upon claims of direct revelation.[45] The earliest literary tradition which designates Moses as prophet, however, is the eighth century northern prophet Hosea (12:14). The Deuteronomic designation of Moses as prophet (Deut 18:15ff., 34:10) then, probably rests on earlier tradition. It is noteworthy that, while the northern narrative tradition (E) presents Moses as oracular figure *par excellence*, it never designates him as prophet.[46] It appears, then, that although Moses is consistently viewed by the northern traditions as oracular figure *par excellence*, this view of him was not universally understood as a specifically prophetic charism. The overwhelming consensus of modern scholars

---

[44]See Mowinckel, *Psalms*, 2. 54-55 and Noth, "Office and Vocation in the Old Testament," in *The Laws in the Pentateuch and Other Studies*, (Philadelphia: Fortress, 1966) 229-49.

[45]For this interpretation see, e.g., H. J. Kraus, *Worship in Israel*, 101ff., and E. W. Nicholson, *Deuteronomy and Tradition* (Philadelphia: Fortress, 1967) 76ff.

[46]Regarding the emphasis on Moses as oracular figure in northern literary traditions, see, e.g., Muilenberg, "The 'Office' of Prophet in Ancient Israel," in *The Bible and Modern Scholarship*, ed. J. P. Hyatt (Nashville: Abingdon 1965) 79ff. Carroll, "The Elijah-Elisha Sagas: Some Remarks on Prophetic Succession in Ancient Israel," *VT* 19 (1969) 400-415; W. L. Holladay, "The Background of Jeremiah's Self-Understanding: Moses, Samuel and Psalm 22," *JBL* 83 (1964) 153-64 and "Jeremiah and Moses: Further Observations," *JBL* 85 (1966) 17-27; von Rad, *Old Testament Theology*, 1. 292ff.; Wilson, "Early Israelite Prophecy," 11ff.

is that Num 12:6-8c pre-dates the composition of Deuteronomy.[47] Hence, it is plausible to suggest that, although Moses appears in Num 12:6-8c as oracular figure *par excellence,* this need not mean that he was viewed as a prophet. This suggestion is supported by the fact that Moses is not designated as a prophet in Num 12:6-8c and also by the fact that the text clearly sets him apart from those who characteristically speak from dreams and visions, i.e., prophets.

Is it possible that behind the proclamation of Num 12:6-8c stand the interests of the Levites in their capacity as mediators of the divine word as that was expressed in the Sinai covenant?[48] According to Exod 32:25-29, the Levites were awarded the priesthood because of their loyalty to the God who had brought the people out of Egypt. According to Deut 33:8-11, the Levites "observed the word and kept the covenant" at Massah and Meribah. Consequently, they received the prerogatives of priesthood, i.e., control of the *urim* and *thummim,* the task of teaching the law, and that of offering sacrifice.[49] Indeed, the overwhelming witness of the Book of Deuteronomy is that guardianship of the covenant and proclamation of its demands were the prerogatives of the Levites (e.g., Deut 17:8-9, 18; 21:5; 27:9f., 14ff.; 31:9-13).[50]

---

[47]See n. 31 above and literature referred to there; also see Kraus, *Worship in Israel,* 105, especially n. 47; Noth, *Pentateuchal Traditions,* 32 (n. 120), 126-27, and *Numbers,* 93.

[48]Von Rad (*Old Testament Theology,* 1. 291) has suggested that this text "could derive from the upholding of the prerogatives of certain priestly functions over against the prophets' reception of revelation." Cf. Coats (*Rebellion in the Wilderness,* 264), who views Moses here as representing Levitical priests although he cites different evidence from mine.

[49]Kraus (*Worship in Israel,* 94ff.) says that the primary task of the Levites was the mediation of covenantal law and that therefore they were viewed as "the Mosaic priesthood." He connects their prominence in oracular activity with worship at the central sanctuaries of the pre-monarchical period. On Levites as covenant mediators, see also G. E. Wright, "The Book of Deuteronomy," in *IB* (1953) 2. 315-16.

[50]In addition, see the role of the Levites in Nehemiah 8, 2 Chr 17:8-9, 30:22, 35:3. Von Rad (*Studies in Deuteronomy* [Chicago: Henry Regnery, 1953] 13-14) says that, although these texts are late, they reflect earlier practice. Nicholson (*Deuteronomy and Tradition,* 76ff.) suggests that the role of covenant mediator which earlier belonged to the Levites was assumed by prophetic circles around the time of Samuel. Cf. Muilenberg, "The 'Office' of Prophet in Ancient Israel," 82-3 on the combination of covenant mediator and prophet.

Can one say that Moses in Num 12:6-8c represents Levites in their capacity as mediators of the covenantal word? It might be objected that Num 12:6-8c does not explicitly bear a covenantal context. While this is true, it must be noted that, in the remaining texts which assert Moses' unique oracular authority, that authority is closely linked with his role as mediator of the covenantal stipulations. This is especially clear in Exod 20:15ff. and Deut 5:4f. While the portrait of Moses in Exod 33:7-11 is not explicitly related to his task as covenant mediator, the parallels between Sinai and the Tent of Meeting as loci for Moses' special revelation as well as the parallels between the derivation of oracular authority from Moses at Sinai (Exodus 18) and at the Tent of Meeting (Numbers 11), show that these texts too connect Moses' special oracular activity at the Tent with his role as mediator of the Sinai revelation.[51] Thus it is plausible to suggest that in Num 12:6-8c Moses represents Levites and that the original purpose of the text was to assert their uniqueness as mediators of God's word. Only Moses (i.e., the Levites) knows God's word directly.

Before looking at the context into which the proclamation of Num 12:6-8c has been placed, it might be helpful to review what has been said thus far in the extended treatment of this unit and its implications for the present study. First of all, it has been argued (pp. 52-54) that Num 12:6-8c is a unit unto itself which was originally independent of the surrounding verses (vv 2-9). This suggests that the prophets of v 6 are not necesssarily to be equated with Miriam and Aaron who appear as antagonists in the controversy of vv 2-9. Secondly, I have tried to show (pp. 54-57) that the proclamation of Num 12:6-8c belongs to a larger cycle of tradition which regarded Moses as unique and superior in relation to others who announce God's word. In addition, I have suggested that the Moses figure here represents the claims of the Levites. The text thus asserts the superiority of Levitical pronouncements (i.e., the mediation of the covenantal word) over prophecy from dreams and visions. In the following pages I hope to

---

[51]R. R. Wilson ("Early Israelite Prophecy," 13, n. 17) seems to doubt the existence of an office of covenant mediator although he posits the existence of prophets whose self-understanding was based on Moses' role as mediator of covenant responsibilities. Deut 18:15ff. links Moses' role as covenant mediator with the designation of prophet. However, I have argued that the designation of prophet here was secondarily linked with the northern tradition of Moses as oracular figure *par excellence*. Deut 34:10 warns against searching too literally for the fulfillment of the promises of a "prophet like Moses." Cf. Muilenburg, "The 'Office' of Prophet in Ancient Israel," 87.

show how a subsequent writer used this portrait of Moses (i.e., the Levite who delivers God's word in a unique and superior way) to settle a later controversy between Levites and Aaronic priests on the question of oracular authority.

NUMBERS 12:2-9
MOSES AND THE PRIESTS

Unlike the other texts which assert the unique oracular authority of Moses,[52] Num 12:6-8c appears in the context of a controversy story. Therefore in order to properly understand Num 12:2-9 and the portrait of Miriam reflected there, the narrative will first be viewed in relation to George Coats' form-critical analysis of the murmuring motif in the wilderness traditions. It will be seen that, while vv 2-9 reflect a general knowledge of this stereotyped motif, the unit also deviates from the original form of the murmuring tradition. The deviation from the original pattern can be explained by pointing to changes in the pattern made by later writers when they added their own stories about controversies in the wilderness. Hence, similarities between Num 12:2-9 and the late controversy about Korah in Numbers 16 will be noted. Finally, I shall examine the content of the particular struggle of Num 12:2-9. On the basis of the form and content of the text, I shall suggest that Num 12:2-9 reflects a struggle between Levites and Aaronic priests over the question of oracular authority.

To my knowledge, the best form-critical and traditio-historical study on the controversy stories in the wilderness narratives is George Coats' *Rebellion in the Wilderness*.[53] Therein Coats has shown that the crises of life in the wilderness (e.g., hunger and thirst) once used to accent positive features of Yahweh's aid, became the framework within which the "murmuring motif" was secondarily placed. In Coats' view, the motif is essentially this: in the wilderness Israel waged a full-scale rebellion against her own election. Fundamentally, the rebellion was voiced as a rejection of Moses' role in leading the people out of Egypt and in the failure of his promise to bring them to a land of milk and honey.

Before examining the relationship of Num 12:2-9 to the murmuring motif, I shall review the two basic formal characteristics of the motif as

---

[52]A possible exception is Num 11:24b-30.

[53]The excellent summaries and references which appear in Carroll's "Rebellion and Dissent in Ancient Israelite Society" can be referred to for a review of recent studies on the rebellion tradition.

Coats has delineated them: (1) The antagonists (the entire community) directly address the leader (Moses alone or Moses and Aaron; sometimes extended to Yahweh, the one whose authority stands behind Israel's leaders) with a question regularly introduced by a negative particle (*lâmâh* or *madû'a*). The purpose of the question is to challenge the leader(s) regarding some past deed. The question implies irresponsibility on the leader's part. (2) The addressee answers with a reason or motivation for the deed challenged by the question. The adequacy of the response rests on showing that Yahweh stands behind the event or person being challenged.

According to Coats, the *Sitz im Leben* for this formal structure lies in the legal process in ancient Israel. That process falls into two stages: (1) Stage 1 consists of an exchange of accusations and counter-accusations by two parties involved in a quarrel. The accusation and counter-accusation appear in the form of questions which challenge the opposition to some kind of explanation for what is regarded as an irresponsible action. This exchange takes place informally, without judge or witness. If the quarrel is not resolved at this stage, there is a transition to Stage 2, the official procedure of appeal before a judge; (2) Stage 2 involves the formal process of law. The parties of the quarrel present their cases publicly and, the case having been heard (sometimes by a repetition of the formal elements of the pre-official stage), a decision is returned.

There are several elements in Num 12:2-9 which not only suggest that the writer knew well the stereotyped motif but also that he used that motif in shaping his narrative.

(1) The questions of v 2 appear as direct quotations as do the questions in the stereotyped motif. In addition, like the motif, the questions are rhetorical in character, i.e., they do not seek information but an explanation (indeed, a defense) of Moses' rights of leadership (in this case, in oracular matters). They imply that Moses has overstepped his rights and therefore they function as accusations.

(2) While the questions are obviously a challenge directed towards Moses' claims to unique oracular authority, like other instances in the murmuring motif,[54] they are presented as ultimately an accusation of Yahweh. This is confirmed by the notation at the end of v 2 that "Yahweh heard" and by Moses' subsequent lack of response.

---

[54] See Coats, *Rebellion in the Wilderness*, 39-40.

(3) Given that the accusation of v 2 was understood as ultimately an accusation against Yahweh, Moses' silence (v 3) is appropriate.[55] However, there is an additional consideration which might stand behind the verse.[56] If the author of Num 12:2-3 knew the formal characteristics of the stereotyped murmuring motif (i.e., the antagonists' question/accusation followed by a response/explanation by Moses) and the legal process from which the form was taken (the exchange of accusation and defense at the pre-official stage of the legal process), Moses' silence in v 3 completes the pre-official stage of the legal process but shows that, at this stage, the dispute is unresolved. As such, it prepares the reader for the movement to the official stage of the legal process (vv 4-5) where the case will be re-presented and settled.

(4) A movement to the official stage of the legal process is suggested by the somewhat belabored account of the transition of the parties involved to the Tent of Meeting. There the antagonists of v 2 are directed to step forward and hear the response to their challenge.[57]

(5) The divine proclamation of vv 6-8 is appropriate since the accusation of v 2 was understood as ultimately directed toward the Divinity. However, its use here also reflects familiarity with the stereotyped motif: (a) Coats has pointed out[58] that a recurring theme in the responses of the stereotyped motif is that it is Yahweh who stands behind the deed (and the person) being challenged. This, of course, is evident in the proclamation of vv 6-8; (b) like responses in the stereotyped motif, vv 6-8 answer the accusation of v 2 by providing a rationale for the point being challenged; (c) vv 6-8 also fit the characteristic form of the legal process.

---

[55] Coats (*Rebellion in the Wilderness*, 38-39) points out that a recurring theme of the stereotyped motif is that before Moses responds to the accusations against him, he falls on his face (signifying his deference in favor of the divine authority against whom the murmuring is really directed).

[56] The verse appears to be a foreign element in the text insofar as it needlessly delays the flow of the dramatic action between vv 2b and 4. Thus Noth (*Numbers*, 95) and Coats (*Rebellion in the Wilderness*, 261) regard it as a later insertion into the narrative. Von Rad (*Old Testament Theology*, 1. 295) links it with the Deuteronomic view of Moses.

[57] The facts that (a) the response comes from Yahweh and (b) only Aaron and Miriam are called to step forward again indicate that the challenge of v 2 was understood as ultimately an accusation of the Divinity.

[58] *Rebellion in the Wilderness*, 39.

Coats says [59] that it is not unusual to find the formal elements of the pre-official stage of the legal process (accusation-response) repeated in the official stage. However, since the author had already noted that "Yahweh heard" the accusation of v 2, there was no need to repeat the challenge. The defense simply states its case.[60]

(6) A particle (the interrogative *madû'a*) which characteristically appears in the accusation of the stereotyped motif introduces the question at the end of v 8. Formally, then, this line must be viewed as an accusation (or rather, as a counter-accusation).[61] The content of the question bears this out. Like the question/accusation of the stereotyped motif, Yahweh's question to Aaron and Miriam does not seek a response. It serves rather to accuse the two of guilt. This is confirmed by the abrupt and definitive end of the dispute: "the anger of the Lord was kindled against them, and he departed" (v 9).

The foregoing analysis of Num 12:2-9 in light of Coats' delineation of the murmuring motif shows that the author of Numbers 12 knew not only the content of the murmuring motif (rebellion against Moses' leadership) but also that he knew its literary form.[62] However, deviations form the original pattern of the murmuring motif also exist in Num 12:2-9:[63] (1) the rebellion against Moses involves individuals and not the entire community as in the stereotyped motif; (2) there is no face-to-face confrontation with Moses as in the stereotyped motif; (3) common lexical characteristics of the questions voiced in the stereotyped motif are missing in Num 12:2-9:[64] (a) the *lâmâh* or *madû'a* of the stereotyped motif has been replaced by the interrogative *hĕ* at the beginning of the question/accusation of v 2; (b) the different interrogative particle

---

[59] *Rebellion in the Wilderness*, 34-35.

[60] If, as suggested above, the proclamation of vv 6-8c at one time circulated independently of the accusation of v 2, this is a further reason which stands behind the lack of a close juxtaposition of the question and response here.

[61] Cf. Coats (*Rebellion in the Wilderness*, 34), who says that, in the official stage of the legal process, "If the defendant's case is strong, he may follow his defense with an accusation of his own (cf. Gen 31:41-42)."

[62] Indeed, he has gone beyond the murmuring motif in presenting a narrative which reflects both the pre-official and the official stages of the legal process.

[63] See Coats, *Rebellion in the Wilderness*, 264.

[64] For a lexical analysis of the murmuring motif, see Coats, *Rebellion in the Wilderness*, 21-28.

removes the need for the infinitive construct which, in the stereotyped motif, follows the principal verb; (c) since there is no face-to-face confrontation with Moses, the second person perfect verbs of the stereotyped motif have been replaced by third person perfect verbs in Num 12:2.

The affinities of Num 12:2-9 with the Korah narrative of Numbers 16 suggest that, like the Korah story, Num 12:2-9 is a later addition to the motif.[65] First of all, the controversy of Num 12:2-9, as in the Korah narrative, is brought forth by individuals and not by the entire community. The fact that Aaron appears to be the principal party in the dispute of v 2-9[66] suggests that, like the Korah story, Num 12:2-9 reflects a late rivalry between priestly groups.[67] Secondly, in the original murmuring motif, the peoples' rebellion against Moses is consistently directed towards his leadership role in bringing them out of Egypt or his continued leadership through the wilderness. Like the controversy over Korah in Numbers 16, Num 12:2-9 bears no such connection with the Exodus or

---

[65]According to Coats (*Rebellion in the Wilderness*, 156-84) Num 16:1b-2aα, 12-15, 24bβ-26, 27aβb-31 is the Dathan/Abiram story, a J narrative which forms the starting point for the stereotyped murmuring motif. All the rest of Num 16-17 is P's adaptation of this early tradition and is designed to assert the rights of Aaronic vs. Levitical priests (cf. von Rad, *Old Testament Theology*, 1. 290). This decision, of course, is in favor of the Aaronides. The last stratum of the story bears resemblance to Lev 10:1-3 (cf. Coats, 257-60; J. C. H. Laughlin, "The 'Strange Fire' of Nadab and Abihu," *JBL* 75 [1976] 559-65 [esp. p. 565, n. 28]). Coats (p. 264) suggests that Num 12:2ff. reflects "the same late period as the material about the conflict between the Levites and the Aaronic priesthood in Numbers 16-17." Cf. Noth, *Numbers*, 93 and G. B. Gray, *Numbers*, 120ff.

[66]Note the change in the order of Miriam and Aaron's names between vv 1 and 4. Codex Vaticanus and Codex Alexandrinus of the LXX, however, retain the word order of v 1 in v 4. Cf. Tunyogi (*The Rebellions of Israel*, 48), who views Aaron as a later insertion into this controversy.

[67]Both Coats (*Rebellion in the Wilderness*, 264) and Cross (*Canaanite Myth*, 204) see vv 2-9 as a conflict within priestly circles. On the other hand, Carroll ("Rebellion and Dissent in Ancient Israelite Society," especially p. 197) views it as a conflict within prophetic circles. The latter opinion is unlikely for two reasons: (1) the antagonists, Aaron and Miriam, are not predominantly prophetic figures, and (2) other prophetic conflicts in the scriptures revolve almost universally (cf. Num 11:24b-30) around the question of false prophecy vs. true prophecy, which, as Num 12:6 indicates, is not the case here. On prophetic conflicts see J. L. Crenshaw, *Prophetic Conflict: Its Effect Upon Israelite Religion* (Berlin: Walter de Gruyter, 1971).

wilderness journey. In voicing questions about Moses' unique authority, both Numbers 16 and Num 12:2-9 presuppose the establishment of a hierarchy in sacral leadership positions which belonged to a late period. The controversy about Korah in Numbers 16 centers upon the question of the legitimacy of the one who approaches the altar. This is not the case in Num 12:2-9. The latter is rather a dispute over who is to render God's word. Both controversies reflect the concerns of priestly groups whose functions included the rendering of the divine word as well as the offering of sacrifice. If there were power struggles regarding legitimacy in approaching the altar (e.g., Numbers 16), then it can be supposed that there were also power struggles among priestly groups regarding the oracular authority of one group versus that of another. The particular content of Num 12:2-9 suggests that the struggle reflected there is precisely over the question of oracular authority. Hence the "trial by oracle"[68] appropriately corresponds to the "trial by sacrifice" of Korah in Numbers 16.

If we are correct in viewing Num 12:2-9 as a conflict between priestly groups over the question of oracular authority, which groups do Moses, Aaron and Miriam represent? It has been shown above (pp. 52-60) that Num 12:6-8c at one time circulated independently and that it was pre-Deuteronomic in origin. Furthermore, it was suggested that in the divine proclamation of Num 12:6-8c Moses represents Levites in their capacity as deliverers of God's word. A later writer, then, had this text available to him and he inserted it into his own composition about a controversy over oracular authority which took place in the wilderness. Within the context of Num 12:2-9 Moses still represents the oracular authority of Levites. Aaron and Miriam on the other hand, appear to represent Aaronic priests. That this is the case is supported by: (1) the fact that Aaron appears to be the principal antagonist in the dispute of vv 2-9;[69] (2) the traditions which

---

[68]W. R. Smith (*Lectures on the Religion of the Semites: The Fundamental Institutions* [1927; reprint 3rd ed., New York: Ktav, 1969] 179) writes: "An oracle that speaks by receiving or rejecting the worshipper and his homage may very readily pass into an ordeal, where the person who is accused of a crime, or is suspected of having perjured himself in a suit, is presented at the sanctuary, to be accepted or rejected by the deity, in accordance with the principle that no impious person can come before God with impunity." In Numbers 12, the oracle and the ordeal are one.

[69]See footnote 66 above.

view Aaron as Moses' mouthpiece (Exod 4:16) and prophet (Exod 7:1),[70] which shows that Aaronic priests might well have been concerned about their rights as oracular authorities; and (3) the fact that elsewhere in the priestly writings Miriam is connected with the Aaronic circle (see chap. 4).

The interpretation of the figures in Num 12:2-9 proposed here alleviates both the problem of trying to understand the place of Aaron in a prophetic controversy and also the problem involved in basing an understanding of Miriam's role in the controversy on the anachronistic notation of Exod 15:20. Coats' suggestion that in Num 12:2-9 Miriam represents prophets and Aaron represents priests is also problematic. First of all, while it is not surprising that a late author (Coats says vv 2-9 is a secondary addition to P) would have represented Aaron as the figurehead for priests, it is unlikely that the same writer would have represented Miriam as the figurehead for all prophets. Secondly, the text of Num 12:2-9 offers no evidence for differentiating the roles of Miriam and Aaron in the controversy. If my analysis is correct, one must suppose that Miriam and Aaron alike represent Aaronic priests in their struggle for authority in oracular matters.

Before proceeding to the final section of this chapter, I shall summarize the results of my study on Miriam "the prophetess" thus far. In the first section of the chapter I showed that, although Miriam is called a prophetess in Exod 15:20, there is little evidence to suggest that the title is anything more than an anachronism. No true prophetic activity is ever attributed to her in the texts. In the section which followed, I tried to show that Miriam's role in Num 12:2-9 is not a prophetic one; rather, in that controversy, she, like Aaron, represents the concerns of Aaronic priests in their struggle with Levites (represented in Num 12:2-9 by Moses) over the question of oracular authority.

Since Num 12:2-9 is closely bound to Num 12:1, 10ff., I shall include a treatment of the remainder of Num 12:1-15 before concluding this chapter.

---

[70]Noth, (*Exodus*, 47) says that Exod 4:13-15 "presents a picture of the messenger of God reminiscent of later 'classical' prophecy." Nevertheless, with regard to its date, he says that the text "represents a secondary addition, made . . . during the transmission of the tradition and perhaps even at the literary stage within the J narrative work" (*Exodus*, 46). Exod 7:1, he says, belongs to the priestly source (*Exodus*, 61-62).

NUMBERS 12:1
MIRIAM AND MOSES' CUSHITE WIFE

According to Num 12:1, the initial subject of Miriam's controversy with Moses was his Cushite wife. Although the Hebrew text says that both Miriam and Aaron confronted[71] Moses on this matter, the verb at the beginning of the verse is feminine singular, suggesting that Aaron was added only after the controversy over the Cushite wife was joined with the second subject of controversy (vv 2ff.).[72]

Num 12:1 is the only text in the scriptures which preserves the tradition that Moses' wife was a Cushite woman. Consequently, the text has long been a puzzle to readers. The final clause of 12:1 indicates that this tradition was not well known even at the last stage of redaction for, after saying that Miriam (and Aaron) complained to Moses on account of his Cushite wife, the text adds the explanatory note "for he had married a Cushite woman."[73]

The Hebrew "Cush" is generally used with reference to Ethiopia,[74] although it also appears to be related to the area of Midian.[75] Since the

---

[71]The Hebrew expression which the RSV translates as "speak against" is *dbr bĕ*. In some contexts (Num 12:8, 21:5, 7; Job 19:18; Ps 50:20; 78:19) the expression certainly bears a meaning of hostile speech. In other contexts, however, the expression is used of Yahweh's speaking through, with or to a person (Num 12:6, 8; 2 Sam 23:2; 1 Kgs 22:28; Hos 1:2; Hab 2:1; cf. Zech 1:9, 13; 2:2, 7; 4:1, 4, 5, 5:5, 10, 6:4). Since, in the latter cases, the subject is always the Divinity, I must agree with the RSV translation in Num 12:1. If the tradition of Miriam's punishment (vv 10) was originally joined to the tradition of 12:1, then this too lends support to the translation given.

[72]See Noth's discussion in *Numbers*, 93. It should be noted, however, that in Hebrew a verb which precedes two subjects might agree in gender and number only with the subject closest to the verb (GKC, 468).

[73]The Vulgate omits the explanatory clause whereas Tg. Onkelos explains Miriam's complaint by saying "because he had sent far away the fair woman he had married." Snaith, *Leviticus and Numbers*, 234; cf. J. Marsh, "The Book of Numbers," in *IB* (1953) 2. 200.

[74]See, e.g., Isa 18:1ff., 20:3; 37:9; 43:3; Jer 13:23; 46:9; Ezek 29:10; 30:5, 9; Nah 3:9. The LXX and the Vg understood the Cushite woman of Num 12:1 to be an Ethiopian.

[75]See, e.g., Hab 3:7. Noth (*Numbers*, 94) understands the Cushite wife as belonging to the area of Midian although, he says, the purpose of the explanatory clause in v 1b is to distinguish this woman from Moses' Midianite wife, Zipporah. Cross (*Canaanite Myth*, 204), on the other hand,

exact meaning of "Cushite" is open to question, it is difficult to determine with any certainty the relationship of the Num 12:1 tradition to those which say that Moses' wife was the Midianite Zipporah (Exod 2:21, 18:2; Exod 3:1, Num 10:29) or a Kenite woman (Judg 1:16, 4:11). Noth plausibly suggests that the variants do not refer to separate foreign wives but rather they they are three mutually independent versions of one of the original elements of the Mosaic tradition, i.e., that Moses had a foreign wife.[76]

Just as the text does not offer the precise identity of the woman in question, so it does not say why she was the occasion for the controversy. One wonders if the objection had roots in a motif which regarded relations with foreign women as occasions for apostasy.[77]

A further problem with Num 12:1 lies in the attribution of the controversy over the Cushite wife to Miriam. Noth says that it was attributed to Miriam because she was "the only female figure in Moses' circle known to tradition."[78] This explanation rests on the assumption that a controversy over a woman must be advanced by another woman. The assumption, of course, is false and so Noth's suggestion does not account for the attribution.

Miriam is not designated as Moses' relative in Numbers 12 (cf. Num 26:59 and 1 Chr 5:29). Moreover, the texts offer no basis for suggesting that a personal rivalry existed between Miriam and Moses' wife.[79] Hence, it seems likely that Miriam is acting as a public figure in Num 12:1 and that, in raising the objection to Moses' wife, she is articulating a matter of public interest. The public nature of her punishment and the fact that

---

identifies the wife of Num 12:1 with Zipporah (whom he calls a Midianite priestess). For other interpretations of the Cushite reference, see G. B. Gray, Numbers, 121-22.

[76] Pentateuchal Traditions, 168-69. Noth goes on to suggest that this tradition probably had its foundation in historical fact.

[77] Cross (Canaanite Myth, 204) regards Num 12:1 as calling into question the legitimacy of the Cushite priesthood because of its "mixed" blood.

[78] Numbers, 94.

[79] If Miriam was regarded as a prophetess, and if, as Haldar has suggested, the wives of Hebrew prophets were also called prophetesses, it is possible that Miriam and Moses' wife were contending for a prophetic position within the community. However, as I have already noted, there is little evidence for suggesting that Hebrew women derived titles or positions from their husbands. Even if this were the case, the text does not offer sufficient information to warrant that this was the problem which lay behind Num 12:1.

the subjects of the rest of the controversies in the wilderness are, without exception, matters of public concern support this suggestion.[80]

In sum, it must be admitted that little can be said with certainty regarding the background and meaning of Num 12:1. Explanations of the identity of the Cushite wife, the reason for the objection to her, and the attribution of the objection to Miriam are all tentative.[81] It is probable that Miriam acts here as a public figure and that she is voicing a public concern. It might be that the concern stemmed from a religious objection to relations with foreign women but this understanding, too, must remain at the level of conjecture.

The fact that Num 12:1 ends with the explanatory remark that Moses had married a Cushite wife has led scholars to regard this verse as stemming from early tradition. If the late writer of Num 12:2-9 had Num 12:1 at his disposal, the two were probably joined by virtue of the fact that both were controversies with Moses and both involved Miriam.[82] In joining the two the late writer effected an ingenious play on words, i.e., Miriam's "speaking against" (*dbr bě*) Moses (v 1; cf. v 8) and Yahweh's "speaking with" (*dbr bě*) the prophets (v 6) and with Moses (v 8).[83] While the Hebrew expression could bear a meaning of *prophetic* speech, in this context, it must be interpreted as *hostile* speech.[84] Hence, the tradition of Miriam and Moses' Cushite wife sheds no light on the tradition which regarded Miriam as a prophetess. The brevity of Num 12:1 and uncertainty about its intent make this line to be of little help in a quest to characterize the

---

[80]As Coats has shown, the real issues of the entire murmuring motif were challenges to Moses' rights in leading the people out of Egypt and/or to the continuation of his leadership.

[81]Noth (*Numbers*, 127), Coats (*Rebellion in the Wilderness*, 263), and Fritz (*Israel in der Wüste*, 77-78) agree that one can no longer be sure what lay behind the controversy of Num 12:1.

[82]Although Aaron appears to be the principal party in the controversy of vv 2-9, there is no evidence that Miriam was not originally part of that controversy too.

[83]According to Coats (*Rebellion in the Wilderness*, 25-26) the expression *dbr bě* occurs as technical terminology in the murmuring motif. He notes, however, that the texts in which it appears are all later additions to the original (J) motif. This confirms my judgment that the writer of Num 12:2-9 knew the murmuring motif and attempted to shape his narrative accordingly when he joined (conflated?) vv 2-9 with Num 12:1.

[84]See note 71 above.

biblical portrait of Miriam. Perhaps it does suggest, as does the portrait of Miriam in Exod 15:20-21, that Miriam was remembered as one who voiced the interests of the entire community.

NUMBERS 12:10-15
MIRIAM'S LEPROSY

The account of Miriam's leprosy poses difficulties for the reader. One problem has to do with the disjunctions in the text. Another deals with the relation of this text to Num 12:1-9.

The account is as follows:

> [10]And when the cloud removed from over the tent, behold, Miriam was leprous, as white as snow. And Aaron turned towards Miriam, and behold, she was leprous. [11]And Aaron said to Moses, "Oh, my lord, do not punish us because we have done foolishly and have sinned. [12]Let her not be as one dead, of whom the flesh is half consumed when he comes out of his mother's womb." [13]And Moses cried to the Lord, "Heal her, O God, I beseech thee." [14]But the Lord said to Moses, "If her father had but spit in her face, should she not be shamed seven days? Let her be shut up outside the camp seven days, and after that she may be brought in again." [15]So Miriam was shut up outside the camp seven days; and the people did not set out on the march till Miriam was brought in again.

The first indication that this is not a smoothly constructed, unified narrative is the fact that the Hebrew text of the Divinity's response in v 14 begins most enigmatically with the *waw* consecutive. If translated literally the line would read:

> And her father surely spitting in her face. Should she not be shamed for seven days?

Kittel is probably correct in suggesting that some words have been omitted at the beginning of this directive. Gesenius cites several other examples where the *waw* consecutive "joins a sentence apparently to what immediately precedes, but in reality to a sentence which is suppressed and which must, therefore be supplied from the context."[85] The context

---

[85]GKC, 485. It is interesting, however, that Gesenius links the omission in Num 12:14 with "passionate excitement or haste which does not allow

allows one to assume that Miriam's subsequent exclusion from the camp is to be regarded as denoting public shame. The custom referred to of spit- ting in the face remains a mystery.

A second disjunction in the text appears in vv 11-12. In the former Aaron appears to share Miriam's guilt and punishment but in the latter he stands merely as a concerned observer to Miriam's plight.[86] One possible explanation for this is to posit that in some layer of tradition now lost, Aaron too was punished.[87] Or, it might be that v 11 was an attempt to link the account of the punishment more closely with vv 2-9. The attempt at harmonization, as can be seen, was not too successful, for in the rest of vv 10-15 there is no allusion to Aaron's share in the wrongdoing or its punishment.

The fact that Miriam alone appears guilty and punished in Num 12:10, 12-15, in my opinion, is best explained by the commonly held view that a tradition of Miriam's leprosy originally followed the early tradition of Num 12:1.[88] As was noted above (p. 67) the verb at the beginning of Num 12:1 is feminine singular, indicating that Aaron was a late addition to the controversy over the Cushite wife. In an early level of tradition, then, Miriam alone initiated a controversy with Moses and she alone was punished with leprosy. The view that Miriam's leprosy is an early tradition is confirmed by my study of Deut 24:8-9 (see chap. 5) where it will be seen that such a tradition circulated prior to the composition of *Urdeuteronomium*. Aaron, then, should be viewed as a late addition to Num 12:10ff.

The early tradition of Miriam's leprosy probably stems more from theological interpretation than from historical fact, for in the scriptures

---

time for full expression." In my opinion, this interpretation is very dubious.

[86]Some (minor) textual witnesses continue the first person plural of v 11 into v 12. The scribes, too, attempted to harmonize the two verses. See Kittel's textual apparatus.

[87]Coats (*Rebellion in the Wilderness*, 262) suggests that the two-fold intercession of vv 11-12 reflects two levels of tradition: one in which Aaron too was punished and another in which only Miriam was punished.

[88]See, for example, Noth, *Numbers*, 92-93 and *Pentateuchal Traditions*, 127, 180. Coats (*Rebellion in the Wilderness*, 262) finds the following strands in Num 12:1-15: (1) the tradition of the Cushite wife, vv 1, 10, 12-16, and (2) the tradition of Moses' unique relationship to Yahweh, vv 2, (3) 4-9, 11. Fritz (*Israel in der Wüste*, 18-19, 75-79) regards Num 12:1, 9aβ, 13-15 as belonging together.

leprosy is widely attested as a divine punishment brought on by some wrongdoing. Thus, according to the Deuteronomic tradition of 2 Kgs 15, the Judean King Azariah (Uzziah) was smitten with leprosy because of his neglect in allowing syncretistic religious practices to continue. The Chronicler (2 Chronicles 26) knew the tradition of Uzziah's leprosy but attributed it to his usurpation of and confrontation over the priestly privilege of burning incense upon the altar. According to 2 Kgs 5 Elisha's servant Gehazi (and all his descendants) were cursed with leprosy because of Gehazi's greed and dishonesty. In 2 Sam 3:29, leprosy is among the curses called down upon Joab by David.[89]

The divine disfavor symbolized by leprosy was normally followed by a censure from the Hebrew community and this usually took the form of isolation. Hence, according to both traditions (2 Kgs 15:5 and 2 Chr 26:21) Uzziah dwelt apart from the community because of his leprosy and, according to 2 Kgs 5:27, Gehazi went out from the presence of Elisha.

In sum, in an early level of tradition, Miriam was remembered as having been wrong in initiating a controversy with Moses over his Cushite wife and consequently suffered the punishment of leprosy sent by the Divinity. According to common custom, her leprosy demanded that she be excluded from the camp.[90] This is the view reflected in those parts of Num 12:10-15 which do not mention Aaron.

Aaron was probably introduced into the punishment story at the same time that the controversy over oracular authority (vv 2-9) was inserted into the early tradition of Miriam's sin (v 1) and punishment (vv 10-15). If Num 12:2-9 is a late composition, as was suggested above, then the addition of Aaron to the punishment story must also be regarded as late. There is evidence in Num 12:10 which suggests that Aaron functions there

---

[89]Cf. Moses' leprosy in Exod 4:6 and the interesting interpretation advanced by E. J. Hamlin, "The Commissioning Ordeal of the Liberator: A Study of Exodus 4:1-9," *Southeast Asia Journal of Theology* 11 (1969) 64-71 (esp. pp. 67-68). In some instances the Hebrew text offers no indication that the disease was the result of divine displeasure. This is true in the cases of the Syrian commander Naaman (2 Kings 5) and of the four unnamed lepers of 2 Kings 7.

[90]Fritz (*Israel in der Wüste*, 77) suggests that an earlier common custom of secluding the diseased person for seven days is given divine legitimation by the (J) author of Num 12:13-15. He sees in Miriam's being "shut up" for seven days technical terminology similar to that of Leviticus 13.

as priest and that, with his appearance in the story, Miriam's punishment
came to be regarded specifically as a case of ritual uncleanness.

Aaron's place in the punishment story and the changes in the significance of Miriam's leprosy which accompanied his inclusion in the story
can be seen when Num 12:10ff. is viewed alongside priestly legislation
regarding leprous persons. That legislation is not so much concerned with
the moral status of lepers as it is with their ritual status. Diseased persons are required to present themselves to a priest for a pronouncement
of ritual uncleanness or cleanness. Specific guidelines by which the priest
is to make this judgment are given in Leviticus 13. Leviticus 14 specifies
purification rites for the person who has been pronounced unclean.

A formal unit which appears no fewer than twenty-five times in Leviticus 13-14 is the following:

(a)   the *waw* consecutive plus the verb "to see" (*r'h*) is
        used to refer to an official examination of the
        diseased person:

(b)   the subject of the verb is the priest;

(c)   the particle *hinēh* with the *waw* consecutive then
        introduces an official statement of the symptom(s)
        observed by the priest;

(d)   an official judgment as to the ritual cleanness or
        uncleanness of the person is made.[91]

The only interruptions in this formal pattern occur in those cases where
the ritual cleanness of the person is not immediately evident.

I shall now view the case of Miriam's leprosy with this legislation in
mind. Num 12:10a says that, after the confrontation with Yahweh at the
Tent, Miriam was "leprous like snow." The analogy "like snow" probably
refers to the white cast of the diseased skin.[92] Of itself, it does not
involve ritual uncleanness.[93] However, according to Leviticus 13, a person

---

[91]In Leviticus 14 the official judgment (d) is sometimes replaced by a
command by the priest as to what action(s) must be performed.

[92]Hence, the RSV translation, "leprous, white as snow." Cf. Snaith,
Leviticus and Numbers, 236.

[93]In fact the expression "leprous, like snow" may have been intended to
distinguish this form of the disease from one which involved ritual
impurity. See, e.g., the frequent use of snow as an analogy for purity (Isa

whose skin has the white cast is required to undergo examination by the priest. If the whiteness appears to be spreading or if it is accompanied by an indentation of the skin, it is a case of ritual uncleanness.

The notation of Num 12:10a is followed by a clause the only apparent purpose of which is to include Aaron in the story. While Num 12:10a tells us that Miriam was "leprous like snow," v 10b adds: "And Aaron turned towards Miriam, and behold, she was leprous." On the surface, Num 12:10b adds no new information. However, when viewed in light of priestly legislation for leprous persons, it is clear that Miriam's leprosy is being examined by Aaron the priest and that it is judged to be a case of ritual uncleanness.

(1)   V 10b begins with the *waw* consecutive in connection with the verb "to turn." This seems to correspond to element (a) in the Leviticus 13 pattern where the verb "to see" is used. Thus Aaron's turning toward Miriam reflects a priestly examination of the leprous person.

(2)   The subject of the verb is Aaron (i.e., the priest). This corresponds to element (b) in the pattern of Leviticus 13.

(3)   A clause beginning with the particle *hineh* with the *waw* consecutive introduces at one and the same time an official statement of the symptoms observed by the priest (element c in the Leviticus 13 pattern) and an official judgment by the priest regarding the ritual status of the diseased person (see element d in the Leviticus 13 pattern). The "and behold, she was leprous" of Num 12:10b, then, represents a conflation of elements (c) and (d) of the Leviticus 13 pattern.[94]

1:18; Job 9:30; Ps 51:9; Lam 4:7). On snow as a symbol for cultic purity in Mesopotamia, see Haldar, *Associations of Cult Prophets,* 204.

[94]Num 12:10 bears remarkable similarity to the Chronicler's account of Uzziah's leprosy. According to 2 Chr 26:19, when Uzziah "became angry with the priests, leprosy broke out on his forehead, in the presence of the priests of the house of the Lord, by the altar of incense" (cf. Num 12:10a). V 20a of 2 Chronicles 26 adds that all the priests "turned, and behold, he (Uzziah) was leprous in the forehead" (cf. the apparent redundancy between Num 12:10a and Num 12:10b). Both Num 12:10b and 2 Chr 26:20a

Setting aside Aaron's statement in v 11, the significance of which can
no longer be understood (see above, pp. 71-72), one sees that when Aaron
is introduced into the early tradition of Miriam's punishment, he appears
there as priest. The likeness of Num 12:10b to priestly legislation regarding leprous persons suggests that Miriam's leprosy, presented simply as
divine judgment in the early tradition, was specified as a case of ritual
uncleanness when Aaron was introduced into the story.[95] According to
priestly legislation, a leprous person who was judged by the priests to be
ritually unclean was required to dwell apart from the community for as
long as the disease remained. In Num 12:12, however, Aaron intercedes
for Miriam, requesting that hers not be a permanent case of ritual
uncleanness and hence that she not be cast out of the community perma-
nently.[96] This intercession allowed the late writer to harmonize his

---

use the verb "to turn" with the waw consecutive (cf. element [a] in the
Leviticus 13 pattern; the RSV has correctly rendered the sense of the verb
of 2 Chr 26:20a by saying that the priests "looked" at Uzziah). As in Num
12:10b, the subject of the verb in 2 Chr 26:20a is the priests. In both Num
12:10b and 2 Chr 26:20a elements (c) and (d) of the Leviticus 13 pattern
have conflated. In each case a clause beginning with the particle hinēh
with the waw consecutive introduces both an official statement of the
symptoms observed by the priest (element [c]) and an official judgment by
the priest regarding the ritual status of the diseased person (element [d]).

[95]In the early tradition Miriam's "shame" (klm) probably did not imply
ritual concerns. Note, however, that in 2 Chr 30:15ff. klm has been
equated with ritual uncleanness. (As far as I can tell, this is the only text
in the Hebrew scriptures where this equation is made.) If the writer who
introduced Aaron into the entire narrative of Numbers 12 had at his
disposal the view that "shame" = ritual uncleanness, it would have been
most natural for him to attach the "shame" associated with the seven-day
exclusion with the tradition of the ritual uncleanness due to leprosy in
Num 12:10b.

[96]Hamlin ("The Commissioning Ordeal of the Liberator," 64-67) points
out similarities between Num 12:12 and initiation rites of shamans.
Hence, he views Miriam's punishment as a symbolic death representing the
renunciation of power. This interpretation certainly fits the context of
Numbers 12. However, the analogy breaks down when one tries to understand Miriam's "ordeal" as a ceremony of initiation by which one becomes
a "technician of the sacred." It is possible, of course, that the tradition of
Miriam's leprosy at one time circulated independently of either of the
controversy stories of Numbers 12. Her leprosy, then, could have been
only a symbolic punishment which preceded initiation to a higher status.
However, it is no longer possible to separate the tradition of Miriam's

account with the earlier tradition that Miriam's leprosy was followed by only a seven-day period of isolation.

SUMMARY AND CONCLUSIONS

This chapter began with a brief survey of biblical texts which witness to the presence of prophetesses in nearly every stage of Hebrew religion. However, unlike Israel's best-known prophetesses, Deborah and Huldah, Miriam is never represented as participating in any true prophetic activity. The writer who is responsible for the designation of Miriam as prophetess in Exod 15:20 (possibly E), then, appears to have used the term anachronistically. In an effort to further identify Miriam in this, her first appearance in the texts, the writer apparently looked to his own times and saw there women religious leaders functioning as prophetesses. Thus, he bestowed this title on Miriam, although, as was seen, neither he nor other biblical writers firmly cast her in this role.

The anachronistic character of the prophetess designation hardly presents a firm foundation upon which to interpret Miriam's role in Numbers 12. Although the present text of Num 12:1-15 is hopelessly conflated,[97] I have attempted to delineate various strata. I suggested that

---

leprosy from the context of Numbers 12. Given the meaning of leprosy in the rest of scripture (with the possible exception of Exod 4:6) and the punishments which inevitably appear in the rest of the controversy stories, one must view Miriam's leprosy as a punishment also.

Von Rad (*Old Testament Theology*, 1. 277) also sheds light on the reference to death in Aaron's plea: ". . . the life of Israel, even the whole of its everyday life, was bounded by a great tension between clean and unclean, between life and death, for every uncleanness was to some extent already a precursor of the thing that was uncleanness out and out, death; in the same way, any slight uncleanness led to death in so far as it was not deliberately wiped out by ritual means."

[97]Noth, *Numbers*, 93; cf. *Pentateuchal Traditions*, 32, n. 120. Fritz (*Israel in der Wüste,* 78) links Num 12:1, 9a, 10a β, 13-15 with the J source. Noth (*Pentateuchal Traditions*, 32, n. 120; cf. 127) tentatively assigns Numbers 12 to the J narrative source because of its consistent use of the divine name Yahweh. He regards Num 12:2-9 as a later expansion of the basic material of J. In his commentary on Numbers, however, he alters his position slightly when he cites problems involved in assigning vv 1, 10ff. to the original J narrative and says: "It is no longer clear where the author of this addition (vv 2-9) found the motif of the reproach against Moses' Cushite marriage" (p. 93). Coats (*Rebellion in the Wilderness*, 263-64)

vv 6-8c once circulated independently and that this text was originally intended to assert Moses' oracular authority over that of prophets who speak God's word out of dreams and visions. This pre-Deuteronomic proclamation of Moses' uniqueness as an oracular figure was subsequently used by a later writer to settle a controversy over oracular authority (vv 2-9) between Aaronic priests (represented by Aaron and Miriam) and Levites (represented by Moses). In Num 12:2-9, then, Miriam is portrayed as an oracular figure but as such she represents a priestly, not a prophetic group.

At some late stage Num 12:2-9 was joined to an earlier tradition (Num 12:1, 10a, 13-15) in which Miriam was portrayed as having raised a question to Moses regarding his Cushite wife and was subsequently punished by the Divinity for this act. The early story and the later controversy (vv 2-9) were probably joined because both were controversies with Moses and Miriam was involved in both. In an effort to harmonize the later tradition with the earlier one, Aaron was added to the controversy over the Cushite wife (v 1) and to the account of Miriam's punishment (vv 10-15). Just as Aaron represents priests in the controversy of vv 2-9, so in his appearance in the leprosy story, he functions as priest who officially declares Miriam's leprosy to be a case of ritual uncleanness. Through his intercession and that of Moses, Miriam's punishment is benevolently handled by the Divinity and she rejoins the wilderness community after a shameful seven-day period of isolation.

The analysis contained in this chapter leads to more negative conclusions than positive ones with regard to the tradition that Miriam was a prophetess.

It is possible that the designation of Miriam as prophetess rests on a larger tradition (not recorded in the texts) which contained a clear and more complete account of her prophetic activity. However, in the absence of such a larger tradition, one cannot assert that the designation of

---

suggests that Num 12:1, 10, 12-16 is a late development in the J narrative but that vv 2 (3), 4-9 and 11 belong to a secondary P source. G. B. Gray (*Numbers*, 124) and R. de Vaux (*Ancient Israel* vol. 2: *Religious Institutions* [New York: McGraw Hill Paperbacks, 1965] 295; Part IV of original edition, *Ancient Israel: Its Life and Institutions,* [New York: McGraw Hill, 1961]) link Numbers 12 with the E source on the basis of the appearance of the "pillar of cloud" at the "tent of meeting." Tunyogi ("The Rebellions of Israel," *JBL* 81 [1962] 385-90), J. Marsh ("The Book of Numbers," in *IB* [1953] 2. 202) and N. H. Snaith (*Leviticus and Numbers,* 234-35) have also linked Numbers 12 with the E source.

Miriam as prophetess (Exod 15:20) was intended to say that she, like Deborah and Huldah, was indeed viewed as a prophetess in Hebrew tradition. From the textual witness about Miriam, it appears best to understand the designation as a loosely-applied anachronistic term which stemmed from a need to define Miriam's role. The answer to this need was provided by the fact that prophetesses did function as authentic oracular figures in various stages of Hebrew religion. This appears to be the origin and proper understanding of the prophetess designation as it was applied to Miriam.

While Num 12:2-9 portrays Miriam as voicing a concern over oracular authority, my analysis of that text leads me to believe that Miriam does so not as a prophetic figure but as a priestly one. This late controversy was joined to an earlier one in which Miriam questioned Moses (v 1) and suffered a resulting punishment (vv 10-15). The early story of Miriam's rebellion against Moses and her punishment is not related to the prophetess designation at all. In confronting Moses over his Cushite wife, there may be an early portrait of Miriam as a leading figure in the community raising a community concern. However, the occasion and significance of the issue she raised is no longer clear. The consequent punishment by leprosy, of course, is implicit witness that the issue was decided by the Divinity in Moses' favor. In the story of Miriam's leprosy and its treatment by the Divinity, a late judgment of ritual uncleanness has been superimposed on an early tradition which portrayed Miriam as shamed but not banished from Hebrew tradition. Her continuing place in the wilderness community is specifically presented as an act of divine clemency.

Regarding the biblical portrait of Miriam as prophetess, I conclude that, although Miriam figures prominently in Num 12:2-9 as an oracular figure, her role there is not specifically a prophetic one. Neither is her activity which is described in Exod 15:20-21 specifically prophetic. When it is said, then, that Miriam was called a prophetess, it must at the same time be admitted that the title is probably anachronistic and hence does not shed much light at all on the portrait of Miriam in the scriptures.

4

Miriam: Sister of Aaron and Moses

The portrayal of Aaron, Moses and Miriam as brothers and sister is, no doubt, the product of a long history of tradition the development of which is difficult to trace. The three are linked in Mic 6:4 but kinship terminology is absent there. They also appear together in the incident recorded in Numbers 12 where Aaron and Miriam are joined as protagonists in a dispute with Moses. However, like Mic 6:4, Numbers 12 does not present the three as brothers and sister. Exod 4:14 says that Moses and Aaron were brothers and Exod 15:20 designates Miriam as Aaron's sister. But the three appear together as brothers and sister only in the Levitical genealogies of Num 26:59 and 1 Chr 5:29.

As is the case in most secondary literature on other texts which mention Miriam, commentators have said little, if anything, about the appearance of Miriam in the texts for consideration in this chapter. Noth has used the designation of Miriam as Aaron's sister as a basis for his view that Exod 15:20f. belongs to the secondary level of the tradition.[1] J. P. Hyatt says that the designation of Miriam as Aaron's sister is probably a gloss secondarily inserted into the J tradition of Exod 15:20-21.[2] On the appearance of Miriam in the Levitical genealogies, Noth[3] simply points out that Num 26:59 is the first time Moses, Aaron and Miriam are linked as brothers and sister in the biblical texts while Gray[4] says that this is the

---

[1]See *Exodus*, 122. Noth's position on the designation of Miriam as Aaron's sister will be discussed in the text of this chapter.

[2]J. P. Hyatt, *A Commentary on Exodus*, 169. Hyatt concludes this because he regards Exod 15:20-21 as belonging to J and notes that Aaron had not yet appeared in the J strand. He does not speculate regarding when or why the gloss was inserted.

[3]Noth, *Numbers*, 209-10.

[4]G. B. Gray, *Numbers*, 396.

only mention of Miriam in P. Curtis and Madsen view Num 26:59 as the source used by the writer of 1 Chr 5:29 when he included Miriam alongside Aaron and Moses as their sister.[5]

The purpose of this chapter is, first of all, to examine Exod 15:20, Num 26:59 and 1 Chr 5:29 with a view to their respective origins. In order to help determine why Miriam was included in the genealogies, specific attention will be given to the overall contexts and purposes of these passages. Secondly, in an effort to clarify precisely what the biblical writers intended when they referred to Miriam as the sister of Aaron and Moses, contemporary research in genealogical texts will be taken into account. Finally, I shall draw some conclusions regarding the significance of these texts for a characterization of the biblical portrait of Miriam.

Because the content and purpose of the genealogical passages which mention Miriam cannot be understood apart from the history of Israel's priesthood, I digress very briefly to present a skeletal outline of major developments within that history.[6]

An ancient Israelite view on priestly personnel is reflected in Judges 17-18. That narrative shows that in pre-monarchical times, Levites were preferred as priests and cultic specialists (although the priesthood was not limited to Levites). At the time of the establishment of the monarchy in Jerusalem, Abiathar (of Levitical origin) and Zadok (a non-Levite) were David's priests (2 Sam 20:25). The latter gained ascendancy over the former to the extent that Levites were eventually denied priestly service in the Temple (1 Kgs 2:35). Tensions between the Levitical group and the Zadokite group came to a head during the Josianic reform. Deuteronomic law (Deut 18:6-7) attempted to assert the rights of Levites by allowing them access to the altar in a priestly capacity. 2 Kgs 23:9 however, indicates that this law failed to take effect.

The Zadokite priests who held positions of power within the Jerusalem establishment were carried off into Babylon along with other influential

---

[5]E. L. Curtis and A. A. Madsen, *A Critical and Exegetical Commentary on the Books of Chronicles*, ICC (Edinburgh: T. and T. Clark, 1910) 128. This possibility will be considered in the pages which follow.

[6]What follows is clearly an over-simplified survey of developments within the Israelite priesthood. For more complete treatments of this subject, see A. Cody, *A History of Old Testament Priesthood*, AnBib 35 (Rome: Pontifical Biblical Institute, 1969); G. B. Gray, *Sacrifice in the Old Testament: Its Theory and Practice* (ed. H. M. Orlinsky; The Library of Biblical Studies; New York: Ktav, 1971) 179-270; de Vaux, *Ancient Israel*, 345-405.

citizens at the time of the Exile. Sometime during this period the Zadokites began calling themselves Levites. However they, like non-Zadokite
Levites of latest pre-exilic Judah, were not yet basing their claims to
priesthood on a genealogical relationship to Aaron (Ezekiel 40-48, for
example, considers Zadokites Levites but Aaron is not mentioned).
After the Exile, the Zadokites returned intending to restore the situation in priestly service which had prevailed in pre-exilic Judah. Upon
returning, however, they were forced to come to terms with some non-
Zadokite Levites who had gained power in Judah during their absence.
Once the Zadokites claimed to be Levites and once they were forced to
recognize the priestly status of these non-Zadokite Levites, a new basis
for distinction in priestly personnel had to be found.

This was the time of widespread preoccupation with genealogies (cf.
Ezra 2:62 and Neh 7:64 where it is shown that anyone who could not bring
proof of his ancestry was excluded from the priesthood). While the Zadokite priests had an ancient ancestor in David's priest, Zadok, the non-
Zadokite priests had begun to base their claims to priesthood on a much
more ancient figure, Aaron. Soon the Zadokites too were claiming relationship to Aaron. By the time of Ezra a compromise was reached: the
Zadokites traced their lineage to Aaron through Eleazar, Aaron's son, and
through Phineas, Aaron's grandson. The non-Zadokites, on the other hand,
claimed descent from Aaron through Eleazar's brother, Ithamar. This
geneaological distinction is standard in the Chronicler's work.

In post-exilic times, then, all priests not only claimed Levitical descent
but also claimed to be "sons of Aaron." In the priestly stratum of the
Pentateuch, Aaron is the first high priest. After the deaths of Nadab and
Abihu (Leviticus 10), Aaron's surviving sons, Eleazar and Ithamar,
remained as the only legitimate priests (Num 3:1-4). Of these two,
Eleazar inherited the high priest's office from Aaron (Num 20:22ff.). The
rest of the members of the tribe of Levi, though connected with cultic
service, were subordinate to Aaron and his sons (Exodus 28-29; Leviticus
8-10; Numbers 16-18).

The above survey is a background for considering those texts which say
that Miriam was Aaron's sister.

EXODUS 15:20

Alongside the designation of Miriam as prophetess in Exod 15:20 there
appears an additional notation which describes her as Aaron's sister. Noth
is of the opinion that this is an early (pre-P) tradition. He says that if

Moses and Aaron were linked as brothers prior to the notation of Exodus 15, Moses "would have had to be mentioned along with Aaron."[7]

I cannot agree with Noth on the date of this notation. Presumably this early writer would have added the notation (that Miriam was Aaron's sister) in order to more specifically introduce her in this, her initial appearance in the texts. However, in the early narrative traditions Aaron was still a rather vague figure.[8] It appears unlikely that an early writer would have introduced an unknown figure by relating her to one who was not well-known.

It seems more probable that the designation of Miriam as Aaron's sister is to be traced to the priestly writer for whom Aaron is not only a prominent figure, but one who is pre-eminently associated with matters of cult. The preceding analysis of Exod 15:20-21 shows that Miriam functions as leader of a cultic celebration in honor of Yahweh, the Divine Warrior. The ritual dance and song which she led clearly recur in later cultic victory celebrations as those are recorded in the texts. Since in post-exilic times all cult officials claimed relationship (expressed in kinship terminology) to Aaron, it seems likely that the designation of Miriam as Aaron's sister represents the priestly writer's (or a priestly editor's) attempt to relate this early "cult official" to Aaron too.[9] If this was the purpose of the additional designation of Miriam, then the inclusion of Moses' name here alongside that of Aaron does not seem so compulsory as Noth assumes.

---

[7]Noth, *Pentateuchal Traditions*, 178; cf. Noth's *Exodus*, 122.

[8]It is not always possible to differentiate early from late sources with regard to Aaron. Scholars are uncertain on the date of the description of Aaron as Levite and Moses' brother; however, it is generally agreed that the early traditions represent him alongside Moses as spokesman (Exod 4:14-16; 17:1-2) and assistant (Exod 5:1-5; 7-10). On the portrait of Aaron in the early traditions, see Cody, *A History of Old Testament Priesthood*, 146-56; de Vaux, *Ancient Israel*, 394-95; de Vaux, *The Early History of Israel* (Philadelphia: Westminster, 1978) 470; and Noth, *Pentateuchal Traditions*, 178-82. It is possible, of course, that Noth is correct in saying that the early tradition about Aaron "contained quite a bit more than what has been retained in the Pentateuchal narrative, which often gives the impression of being only the fragmentary remains of a richer narrative material" (*Pentateuchal Traditions*, 181).

[9]It is noteworthy that the designation of Miriam as Aaron's sister is more appropriate to the context of Exod 15:20-21 than is the description of her as prophetess for, as was pointed out in chap. 3, Miriam's celebration is not specifically prophetic in character.

NUMBERS 26:59

Num 26:59 goes beyond Exod 15:20 in saying that Miriam was viewed as the sister of both Aaron and Moses. In order to understand the significance of the inclusion of Miriam in this line, it is necessary to view the larger context of the passage.

Numbers 26 consists of the names of the descendants of Jacob's sons listed by families together with the total number which belonged to each family. The purpose of the list, according to v 2, is to ascertain the military strength of the tribes,[10] although in another stratum of tradition (vv 52-56) the same lists are said to have been a basis for the allotment of the land of Canaan among the tribes. Whatever purposes the lists may actually have served, Johnson is undoubtedly correct in saying that, as they now appear in the text, the lists of Numbers 26 serve a specifically religious purpose. That is to say, the chapter

. . . purports to show the identity of the people of the exodus with families of the patriarchs . . . thus affirming the status of the Israelites in Palestine as "sons of Abraham" and therefore the true heirs of God's promises to the patriarchs.[11]

There are elements in the text which suggest that the material about the Levites (vv 57-62) at one time circulated independently of the rest of the tribal list.[12] A glance at the text of Numbers 26 shows that the material about the Levites is set apart from the rest of the chapter by the intrusion of vv 52-56, the tradition which says that the land was to be alloted according to the families which had just been listed. The reason for the separate treatment of the Levites, according to v 62, is "because there was no inheritance given to them among the people of Israel."[13] Num 26:62, then, presupposes the addition of vv 52-56 to the chapter.

---

[10]See G. E. Mendenhall, "The Census Lists of Numbers 1 and 26," *JBL* 77 (1958) 52-66.

[11]M. D. Johnson, *The Purpose of Biblical Genealogies*, SNTSMS 8 (Cambridge: Cambridge University, 1969) 44.

[12]Noth (*Numbers*, 202) has advanced the likelihood that the entire chapter consists of originally independent units.

[13]The section on the Levites also stands apart from the rest of the list on lexical grounds. Whereas the families of the rest of the sons of Jacob are introduced with *běnê šimě'ôn, běnê yěhûdāh*, etc., the Levitical material begins with *'ēleh pěqûdê halēwî*.

In incorporating the material about the Levites, the compiler of Numbers 26 asserts that, like the rest of the tribes, Israel's priestly family had roots in the patriarchal period. Even though they did not inherit a portion of the land, the Levites genuinely belonged to the theological entity of the people of Israel. A close look at the Levitical material in Num 26:57-62 shows that the passage is not a compact unity. The text reads as follows:

> [57] These are the Levites as numbered according to their families: of Gershon, the family of the Gershonites; of Kohath, the family of the Kohathites; of Merari, the family of the Merarites. [58] These are the families of Levi: the family of the Libnites, the family of the Hebronites, the family of the Mushites, the family of the Korahites. And Kohath was the father of Amram. [59] The name of Amram's wife was Jochebed the daughter of Levi, who was born to Levi in Egypt; and she bore to Amram Aaron and Moses and Miriam their sister. [60] And to Aaron were born Nadab, Abihu, Eleazar and Ithamar. [61] But Nadab and Abihu died when they offered unholy fire before the Lord. [62] And those numbered of them were twenty-three thousand, every male from a month old and upward; for they were not numbered among the people of Israel, because there was no inheritance given to them among the people of Israel.

The verses appear to be a combination of three different strata of tradition: (1) vv 57 and 62; (2) v 58a; and (3) vv 58b-61. First of all, in naming the Levitical families and giving their total number,[14] the verses which frame the unit (vv 57 and 62) in a general way bear similarity to the pattern of the rest of Numbers 26. I suggest that it was the writer of these verses and of vv 52-56 who incorporated the Levitical material into the rest of the chapter. This writer, however, utilized material from two other sources.

It is immediately apparent that the list of Levitical families which appears in v 58a differs from that of v 57. This discrepancy suggests that two sources have simply been juxtaposed with no effort at harmonization. The absence of genealogical terms in v 58a and the apparent absence of a connection with any persons named in the surrounding unit warrant setting it aside as a separate, probably ancient, [15] tradition.

---

[14] For a different numbering of Levites, see Num 3:39.

[15] Noth, *Numbers*, 209 and G. B. Gray, *Numbers*, 395.

Vv 58b-61 seem to come from still another source.[16] While Kohath (v 58b) forms the connecting point between v 57 and 59, the two lines are marked by a change of form (v 57 simply has a list while vv 58b-61 might be called a "genealogical narrative" form[17]) and also by a change of focus from families (v 57) to individuals (vv 58b-61). Vv 58b-61, with its focus on individuals, must have originally served a different purpose than the verses which frame it (vv 57 and 62) for the naming of these individuals has little bearing on the list of Levitical families and their total number. Another reason for separating vv 58b-61 from vv 57 and 62 is that in vv 58b-61 two women (Jochebed and Miriam) are included in the Levitical genealogy. But the total numbering of the children of Levi given in v 62 is specifically said to represent "every male (zkr) from a month old and upward." Just as the final writer was lax in ironing out the discrepancy between the lists in vv 57 and 58a, so he neglected to harmonize the details of vv 58b-61 and v 62, the latter exclusively numbering males and the former including two females.

Having viewed the overall context and purpose of Numbers 26, and having isolated the verses of special interest for this study, I am now prepared to examine the purpose and origin of the passage which mentions Miriam, Num 26:58b-61.

The aim of vv 58b-61 seems to be that of tracing a direct lineage from Kohath through Amram and Aaron to Aaron's surviving sons. Kohath, of course, serves as the connecting link between vv 57 and 59. The fact that Gershon and Merari's descendants are not named indicates a special interest in Kohath. Whereas other genealogical texts (e.g., Exod 6:18; Num 3:27, etc.) say that Kohath had four sons, here only Amram is mentioned. Of Amram's three children (Aaron, Moses, Miriam), Aaron is singled out for special attention insofar as only his sons are named. Eleazar and Ithamar are singled out by a process of elimination (v 61). The special interest shown in the vertical relationships surrounding Aaron

---

[16]See G. B. Gray, *Numbers*, 395.

[17]On the narrative form used here, see Wilson, *Genealogy and History in the Biblical World*, Yale Near Eastern Researches 7 (New Haven: Yale University, 1977) 139 and sources cited there. In naming Miriam last and in adding the notation that she was their sister (a superfluous piece of information to the modern reader since the three have the same parents), the writer appears to be following a stylized pattern according to which "sisters" are included in biblical genealogies. See, e.g., Gen 36:22; Gen 46:17; 1 Chr 3:9b, 19b; 1 Chr 4:3b; 1 Chr 7:32, etc.

reflects the work of one who was concerned to trace the priestly line from Aaron and ultimately from Levi.

If tracing the one line—from Levi and Aaron to Aaron's surviving sons —is the primary purpose of this text, why does the genealogy branch off to include figures who do not fall directly into that line, namely Jochebed, Moses and Miriam? The answer probably lies in the "all Israel" orientation of Numbers 26. If the purpose of Numbers 26 was to show that all the people of Israel had roots in the patriarchal generation, then it was to the writer's benefit to stress that Jochebed herself authentically belonged to the patriarchal family (v 59a),[18] to include the major figures of the next generation (Moses and Miriam), and to end the list with both Eleazar and Ithamar, the two to whom all post-exilic priests (Zadokites and non-Zadokites) traced their ancestry.

It is difficult to say whether Jochebed, Moses and Miriam were included in the Levi-Kohath-Amram-Aaron-Eleazar/Ithamar genealogy of vv 58b-61 prior to its incorporation into Numbers 26. If so, the purpose of their appearances in the simple list of Israel's priests is difficult to explain. It is very possible that these "extras" were added only when the Levi-Kohath-Amram-Aaron-Eleazar/Ithamar lineage was brought into Numbers 26 and that they were added in order to enhance the overall purpose of the compiler of Numbers 26.

A comparison of Num 26:59 and Exod 6:20 shows that such additions could be made to genealogies.[19] When the two texts are viewed side by side, the similarities as well as the differences are striking.

Exod 6:20:	Num 26:59:
Amram took to wife Jochebed his father's sister	The name of Amram's wife was Jochebed the daughter of Levi who was born to Levi in Egypt and she bore to Amram
and she bore him Aaron and Moses.	Aaron and Moses and Miriam their sister.

---

[18]The mother of Aaron, Moses and Miriam is named only here and in Exod 6:20. It is interesting to note that, according to Num 26:59, Aaron is actually more closely related to Levi through his mother than through Amram. That is, through Jochebed Aaron is Levi's grandson whereas through his father he is Levi's great-grandson.

[19]This phenomenon of "fluidity" in genealogies is discussed by R. Wilson, *Genealogy and History, passim*.

If Noth is correct in saying that Num 26:59 is later than Exod 6:20,[20] the two discrepancies between the texts must be accounted for, i.e., the different descriptions of Jochebed and the addition of Miriam in Numbers 26.[21] The differences can be traced to the respective purposes of the two texts.

The fact that the Levitical genealogy of Exod 6:16-25 ends with the singling out of Eleazar through the naming of his son, Phinehas, indicates that this genealogy (unlike Num 26:57-62) was the special property of the Zadokite priests. The repeated mention of the wives (including their lineage) of the chief Levitical figures in Exod 6 suggests that the primary goal of that writer was to establish the full legitimacy of Israel's chief priests by citing their maternal heritage.[22] It is possible that the genealogist of Exodus 6 knew Miriam and the tradition that she was the sister of Aaron and Moses; however, this detail did not fit the overall purpose for which his genealogy was constructed and therefore it was omitted.

The genealogist of Num 26:59 may have changed the description of Jochebed from Amram's "father's sister" (Exodus 6) to "daughter of Levi who was born to Levi in Egypt" (Numbers 26) for reasons which stem from his particular purpose. The identification in Numbers 26 more explicitly identifies Jochebed with the people of Jacob's sons. This is a significant detail if the overall purpose of Numbers 26 was to relate the Israelite nation to its patriarchal origins.[23] Likewise, the addition of Miriam

---

[20] *Numbers*, 209.

[21] Although Miriam is not mentioned in the MT of Exod 6:20, Kittel's textual apparatus shows that the Samaritan and LXX versions include her. They say that Jochebed bore "Aaron, Moses and Miriam their sister." This, no doubt, was a scribal effort to repair the discrepancy between Exod 6:20 and Num 26:59. The Syriac also includes Miriam, listing her before Moses (Jochebed bore "Aaron, Miriam and Moses"). In changing the order of the names, the scribe here seems to have in mind Miriam's primary association with Aaron (cf. Exod 15:20 and possibly Numbers 12).

[22] According to the legislation for the priest "who is chief among his brethren" (Lev 21:10ff.), only the chief priest was required to "take to wife a virgin of his own people" in order that "she may not profane his children among the people." According to Lev 21:7, other priests were not bound by this requirement. See M. D. Johnson's discussion (*The Purpose of Biblical Geneaologies*, 87-99) of post-biblical concerns regarding the pedigree of Jewish wives and mothers.

[23] The description in Num 26:59 also blurs the tradition that Amram married his "father's sister" and may be related to the directive of Lev

enhances the "all Israel" orientation of Numbers 26 and thus fits that writer's purpose.

The inclusion of Miriam in Num 26:59, then, is best understood as a creative addition on the part of the genealogist. In branching off from the Levi-Kohath-Amram-Aaron-Eleazar/Ithamar line, the writer has effectively presented to the people of Israel a comprehensive sweep of major figures from the patriarchal and exodus-wilderness generations.

The Num 26:59 tradition that Miriam was the sister of both Aaron and Moses must stem from a late period. The passage presupposes that all Israel's priests not only claimed to be Levites but also Aaronides.[24] Also, the fact that details regarding the deaths of Nadab and Abihu were known (v 61) indicates that the unit which mentions Miriam stems from a time when the Pentateuchal narratives were known more or less in their final form. If, in the narrative tradition, Moses and Aaron were already thought to be brothers (Exod 4:14) and, if the priestly tradition had already designated Miriam as Aaron's sister (Exod 15:20), it would have been a small step for a genealogist to link the three wilderness leaders together in a kinship filiation.[25]

The fact that Miriam appears within the context of a lineage traced from Levi through Kohath and Aaron to Eleazar and Ithamar indicates that the memory of Miriam was perpetuated within priestly circles. Miriam's lineage was certainly not of prime importance to this genealogist. Nevertheless, the writer includes her and this indicates that post-exilic priestly circles recognized her as an authentic religious figure belonging to their ancient past.

20:20 which prohibits a man from lying with his aunt (dōdātô). The two possible explanations for the change need not be mutually exclusive.

[24]In ending with Eleazar and Ithamar (Num 26:60-61), the passage is roughly contemporary with the time of Ezra when all legitimate priests claimed one or the other as ancestors.

[25]Noth (Numbers, 204) is of the opinion that vv 52-56 were added to Numbers 26 after the P redaction of the Pentateuchal narratives. It belongs, he says, to a later period "when the Pentateuchal narrative was being revised preparatory to being joined to the deuteronomistic historical work." The Levitical material (vv 57-62) must also be that late since, as was noted above, v 62 presupposes the insertion of vv 52-56.

1 CHRONICLES 5:29[26]

The work of the Chronicler is prefaced with nine chapters of genealogical lists. The opening chapter of the unit traces the descendants of Adam and the closing one lists those who returned from exile. The intervening material (chaps. 2-8) traces in detail the descendants of Israel (Jacob). Within chaps. 2-8 the special attention given to the families of Judah and Levi reflects the Chronicler's theological bias in favor of the southern kingdom and the Davidic line on the one hand, and his preoccupation with the Temple and cult personnel on the other hand. For the Chronicler, these form the basis for the post-exilic theocracy.[27]

The Levitical genealogy (1 Chr 5:27ff.) traces the lineage of post-exilic cultic personnel, all of whom claim Jacob's son, Levi, as ancestor. At the head of the Levitical material stands the genealogical listing of Israel's chief priests. It is this genealogy of the chief priests which includes Miriam.

In the genealogy of the chief priests, several names appear in each of the early generations:

> The sons of Levi: Gershom,[28] Kohath, and Merari.
> The sons of Kohath: Amram, Izhar, Hebron and Uzziel.
> The children[29] of Amram: Aaron, Moses and Miriam.

---

[26]Note that the RSV follows the LXX enumertion of verses in which this is 1 Chr 6:1.

[27]On the theological purpose of the Chronicler, see esp. the introductory section of J. M. Myers, *I Chronicles*, AB (Garden City, New York: Doubleday and Company, 1965); see also Freedman, "The Chronicler's Purpose," *CBQ* 23 (1961) 436-42; R. J. Coggins, *The First and Second Books of the Chronicles*, The Cambridge Bible Commentary (Cambridge: Cambridge University, 1976) 6-7; and R. J. North, "Theology of the Chronicler," *JBL* 82 (1963) 369-81.

[28]The Chronicler regularly spells this name with a final *mem* whereas Pentateuchal sources use the final *nun*. In the RSV translation "Gershom" appears here. This is a departure from the MT. No doubt the translators intended to bring this text in line with other appearances of the name in Chronicles.

[29]The MT uses *bĕnê* throughout these verses. Literally the word means "sons" although it is commonly used in the scriptures to refer to males and females alike. The RSV translators recognize that the inclusion of Miriam here rules out the literal translation. J. Myers (*I Chronicles*, 45) notes the problem with the literal translation. He raises the possibility that Miriam

The sons of Aaron: Nadab, Abihu, Eleazar and Ithamar.
(vv 27-29)

Beginning with v 30 only one son of each generation is named:

Eleazar was the father of Phinehas,
Phinehas of Abishua,
Abishua of Bukki . . .

The list ends with the name of Jehozadak, the chief priest who was carried into exile.

The content of the genealogy points directly to its purpose: Israel's chief priests traced lineage to Zadok and through him to Eleazar. Thus the lineage which was unique to the chief priests appears only in vv 30-41. However, relationship to Aaron and ultimately to Levi were necessary qualifications for all priests during the post-exilic period. Thus, the information contained in vv 27-29, though not unique to the Zadokites, was a necessary part of their genealogy.

The content of vv 27-29 helps to clarify the significance of the mention of Miriam within this genealogy. The purpose of the genealogist as described above would have been met had only Levi, Kohath, Amram, Aaron and Eleazar been named in the early generations. What appears, however, is a more or less complete list of all the children in each of the generations as known in the Pentateuchal traditions. Miriam is included here as part of the genealogist's effort to present a comprehensive list of the Levites prior to Eleazar. She appears along with others who do not exercise a direct influence on the lineage of the chief priests but who nevertheless were significant figures in Israel's ancient ancestry. While Miriam was not of special importance in the Zadokite lineage, the fact that she is included witnesses to the tenacity of her place in Israel's memory.

The names in the first four generations and the order in which they appear are generally consistent with Levitical genealogies in the Pentateuch,[30] although this text is not an exact reproduction of any one Penta-

---

was a later addition to the text. However, in my opinion, there is little to recommend this suggestion.

[30]It is widely agreed that the genealogies of 1 Chronicles 1-9 are derived from the completed tetrateuch and the Deuteronomic history. It is also possible that the author made use of other lists. On the Chronicler's use of sources, see Myers, *I Chronicles*, xlix-lxii; M. D. Johnson, *The*

teuchal genealogy (cf. Gen 46:11; Exod 6:16ff.; Num 3:1-3; Num 26:57-62). In including Miriam the Chronicler was without doubt relying on Penta- teuchal tradition though it would be difficult to trace a direct dependence on Num 26:59, the only other text which links Aaron, Moses and Miriam as brothers and sister. First of all, the narrative form used in Num 26:59 does not appear in 1 Chr 5:29.[31] Secondly, Jochebed does not appear in 1 Chronicles 5 as she does in Numbers 26. Finally, whereas 1 Chronicles 5 lists Amram's brothers, Numbers 26 does not. It is clear, then, that the writer of 1 Chronicles 5 was not simply copying Pentateuchal tradition.

The fact that 1 Chr 5:29 does not exactly reproduce Num 26:57-62 indicates that the writer of 1 Chr 5:29, like the writer of Num 26:59, made a deliberate choice to include Miriam in his genealogy.[32] Besides Num 26:59, the writer of 1 Chr 5:29 presumably had access to the Penta- teuchal tradition of Exod 6:20. The information contained in the Levitical genealogy of Exodus 6 bears close similarity to that contained in 1 Chr 5:27-29 with two notable exceptions; (1) 1 Chronicles 5 does not include the wives of Amram, Aaron and Eleazar while Exodus 6 does; (2) the Chronicles text includes Miriam but Exodus 6 does not.

As in the case of Num 26:59 and Exod 6:20, the discrepancies between Exod 6:20 and 1 Chr 5:29 are best explained by the respective purposes of the two genealogists. For the writer of 1 Chr 5:27ff., the maternal lineage of Israel's chief priests was not an issue as it was for the writer of Exodus 6. Therefore, he did not include the wives of the early Levitical figures, although he may have had access to this information. On the other hand, as was said above, the genealogist of 1 Chr 5:27ff. was concerned to present a comprehensive coverage of the earliest generations of the Zadokite lineage. Therefore he included Miriam as a contribution to that purpose even though the tradition of Exodus 6 did not mention her.

In presenting Miriam as the sister of Aaron and Moses, the writer of 1 Chr 5:29, then, was probably relying on earlier tradition. However, a comparison of this text with the Levitical genealogies of Num 26:59 and

---

Purpose of Biblical Genealogies, 51, 55-57; and Coggins, *The First and Second Books of the Chronicles,* 9-10.
    [31]The Chronicler, however, knew the narrative form. See, e.g., 1 Chr 1:50; 2:3-4; 2:18-19, etc.
    [32]Again, genealogists could exercise some degree of creativity in constructing a genealogy when this would serve the purpose for which the genealogy was drawn up. The most notable example of this is the fact that in 1 Chr 6:18 Samuel is given a Levitical ancestry even though earlier tradition (1 Sam 1:1) said that he was an Ephraimite.

Exod 6:20 shows that he was not simply copying Pentateuchal sources. The fact that the writer of 1 Chr 5:29 chose to include Miriam indicates that she continued to be an active figure in Israel's religious memory at least until c. 400 B.C. or perhaps even later.[33]

Summarizing what has been said thus far with regard to the origin of the texts which link Miriam in a kinship relationship with Aaron or with Aaron and Moses, I have suggested that, of the three texts under consideration, the designation of Miriam as Aaron's sister in Exod 15:20 is the earliest. However, it should not be dated too early. Rather, it is best seen as belonging to a priestly redaction of the Pentateuch which was eager to connect Aaron with all early cultic figures. This situates the text firmly in the post-exilic period. Likewise, the mention of Miriam in Numbers 26 should be traced to a post-exilic priestly genealogist. The inclusion of both Eleazar and Ithamar in that passage may suggest that it was roughly contemporary with the time of Ezra for Ezra 8:2 reflects the distinctions between priests who claimed ancestry in Eleazar (through Phinehas) and those who claimed ancestry in Ithamar. If this is the case, Num 26:59 probably comes from the latter part of the fifth century. Finally, the mention of Miriam in 1 Chr 5:29 comes from the Chronicler or from a later editor of the Chronicler's work.

It appears likely that Miriam owes her place in the genealogies of Israel's post-exilic priests to the Pentateuchal tradition that she was Aaron's sister. The tradition that she was Aaron's sister, in turn, rests on her leadership in cultic activity. The ancient tradition of her ritual dance and song in Exod 15:20-21 formed the basis for her inclusion in Aaron's family. In other words, she was called Aaron's sister *because* she was regarded as a cult leader and not vice versa. This leads us to a further question: if relationship to Aaron had never become the decisive factor in determining who were Israel's legitimate priests (i.e., if the early figure of Aaron had developed in a non-priestly direction or had not developed at all), would Miriam have still have included in Levitical genealogies? In other words, was the post-exilic period the starting point for the tradition which gave Miriam a Levitical ancestry?

---

[33]Scholars do not agree on the origin of the genealogical introduction in 1 Chronicles 1-9. On the one hand, M. D. Johnson (*The Purpose of Biblical Genealogies*, 44-55) and Coggins (*The First and Second Books of the Chronicles*, 9) say that it belongs to the Chronicler himself. On the other hand, W. A. L. Elmslie ("The First and Second Books of Chronicles," *IB* [1954] 3. 394ff.), de Vaux (*Ancient Israel*, 390), and Myers (*I Chronicles*, xli) attribute the nine chapters to a later editor.

Unlike Moses and Aaron, Miriam has no explicit relationship with the Levites in the Pentateuchal narratives.[34] My analysis of Num 20:1, however, will show the connection between Miriam and Kadesh. If the Levites too had connections with Kadesh, as they seem to have had,[35] it might well be that Miriam was claimed by the Levites in an early period and apart from her genealogical connection with Aaron. The fact that Miriam functioned as a cult official in the ancient tradition of Exod 15:20-21 offers a second basis for suggesting that her Levitical connections go back to pre-exilic times, for before cult officials began to claim Aaron as an ancestor, the Levites were thought to have pre-eminence in matters of cult. During the period when Levites were preferred as cultic officials (cf. Judges 17-18) and certainly by the time that cult officials were restricted to the family of Levi, it would have been natural to include Miriam in the Levitical family. In light of this, the post-exilic texts of Num 26:59 and 1 Chr 5:29 may indeed reflect early tradition in including Miriam in the Levitical family although the absence of early textual witness to this effect makes it impossible to say this with certainty.

Finally, what do these genealogical texts say about the portrait of Miriam as she was remembered in the post-exilic era? First of all, it is widely agreed by contemporary scholars that biblical genealogies reflect much more about functional relationships between individuals and groups than about actual biological ties.[36] This is succinctly stated by Robert Wilson:

> Our work on biblical, as well as extrabiblical, genealogies indicates that genealogies are not normally created for the purpose of conveying historical information. They are not intended to be historical records. Rather, in the Bible, as well as in ancient Near Eastern literature and in the anthropological material, genealogies seem to have been created and preserved for domestic, politico-jural and religious purposes,

[34]Exodus 2 tells us that Moses' parents were of the house of Levi and Exod 4:14 designates Aaron as a Levite.

[35]On the Levites and Kadesh, see von Rad, *Old Testament Theology*, 1 p. 12 and especially R. B. Robinson, "The Levites in the Pre-Monarchical Period," in *Studia Biblica et Theologica* 8 (1978) 3-24.

[36]For a review and critique of recent research on biblical geneaologies, see Wilson, "The Old Testament Genealogies in Recent Research," *JBL* 94 (1975) 169-89.

and historical information is preserved in the geneaologies only incidentally.[37]

In light of the purposes of both Num 26:57-62 and 1 Chr 5:27ff. which were discussed above, it is clear that these genealogies contain a statement about Miriam's place specifically in the religious sphere and not, for example, in the social or political sphere.[38] In linking Miriam with Aaron and Moses, the genealogical texts indicate that Miriam was viewed as a religious leader alongside the two. The genealogists have used kinship terminology to express what is essentially the same portrait of Miriam reflected in Num 12 and Mic 6:4.

Secondly, the fact that Miriam is said to be Aaron and Moses' sister (and not mother, daughter, niece, etc.) helps to clarify her status vis-à-vis that of Moses and Aaron in the eyes of the post-exilic community. Wilson has shown that in the formation of genealogies, primary kinship filiations in the same generation express a relationship of parallel status.[39] The status expressed by the brothers-sister relationship of Aaron, Moses and Miriam applied, of course, to their respective places in Israel's general religious heritage and not to status which was specifically priestly in character. The fact that Aaron occupies a special place in the genealogies surrounding both appearances of Miriam in Num 26:59 and 1 Chr 5:29 indicates that, in a specifically priestly role, he was indeed superior to both Moses and Miriam.[40] Nevertheless, the genealogical texts indicate

---

[37] Wilson, *Genealogy and History*, 199.

[38] Cf. the place of the wives and concubines of Jacob whose functions in genealogies probably were intended to express political or social relationships among the tribes.

[39] Wilson, *Genealogy and History*, 195; cf. p. 32 in the same work on Wilson's anthropological research: "The degree of filiation involved is frequently implied in the kinship relation by means of which the genealogical connection is made. For example, the person who is joined as 'brother' has a higher status than one filiated as 'son' or a 'sister's son.' In this case, the genealogy is a generally accurate reflection of the person's position in the society, and it may indicate the degree to which he actually shares all the rights and obligations accompanying group members." It is difficult to know with certainty whether what is true of the relationship of "brothers" is also true of "brother-sister" relationships. That Miriam is "sister" to the two at least suggests a high status and one which was in some way parallel to Moses and Aaron.

[40] Numbers 12, of course, distinguishes between the relative (priestly) status of the three in favor of Moses.

that Miriam was viewed as a figure in Israel's ancient religious heritage parallel with Moses and Aaron, even though Levitical priesthood was ultimately passed on only through Aaron.

Thirdly, the significance of Miriam's inclusion in these genealogies can be seen when the textual witness is viewed against the general background of the place of women in biblical genealogies.[41] Women are rarely named in biblical genealogies. This, of course, is not so much a reflection of the female population of ancient Israel as it is a commentary on their position (or lack thereof) in patriarchal society, politics and religion. When they do appear in genealogical texts, their significance rests largely on their roles as wives or mothers of important figures.[42] Miriam is an exception to this general pattern. The biblical texts reflect no memory of a husband or son(s) from whom her significance derived. If the texts which relate her to Aaron and Moses are late, as they seem to be, one must suppose that, prior to being brought into this family circle, she had attained a significance in Israel's religious tradition which was originally independent of them. The fact that she is included in the family circle as "sister" and not as mother, wife or daughter probably attests to this.[43]

Fourthly, it has been shown that the writers who included Miriam in Num 26:59 and 1 Chr 5:29 were active transmitters of a tradition about Miriam. That is to say, in including her they do not seem to have been merely copying texts at their disposal. The fact that one of the genealogical texts appears in the Book of Chronicles indicates that the memory of Miriam was alive during the latest periods of composition of the canonical books.

Finally, who were the writers who included Miriam in the texts which have been considered in this chapter? They were groups preoccupied with

---

[41]The place of women in biblical genealogies is a relatively unexplored area in biblical research. It is possible that future studies in this area will modify my conclusions regarding what the genealogical texts say about the biblical portrait of Miriam.

[42]On the female figures in the patriarchal narratives, see Noth, *Pentateuchal Traditions*, 149-51. On related topics, see, e.g., W. R. Smith, *Kinship and Marriage in Early Arabia* (London: A. and C. Black, 1903; reprint ed., Boston: Beacon Press, n.d.) esp. pp. 1-39; and Karin R. Andriolo, "A Structural Analysis of Genealogy and Worldview in the Old Testament," *American Anthropologist* 75 (1973) 1657-69.

[43]To my knowledge, Miriam is the only woman named in post-exilic genealogies of the Aaronic priesthood who is not someone's wife or mother.

the legitimacy of cultic personnel and they were groups for whom Aaron, specifically as priest, was a pivotal figure. In light of the general absence of women in high-ranking religious and cultic positions in Israel's history, Miriam's appearance here is remarkable. The apparent absence of women in official priestly positions makes the designation of Miriam as Aaron's "sister" all the more remarkable.

MIRIAM: PRIESTESS?

The above leads to the question of whether or not Miriam was portrayed as having exercised a priestly role in ancient Israel.

Miriam belonged to a world where women commonly held positions which were priestly in character.[44] One would naturally expect to find priestesses in Israel as well. However, the Hebrew texts never use the feminine with reference to "priest" and, once the offering of sacrifice came to be the prerogative of priests, women are never portrayed as functioning in this capacity on behalf of Israel's worshipping community. Moreover, Gray has noted that "the physical disabilities of priestly service are expressed in terms inapplicable to and irrelevant to women."[45] The silence of the texts on the question of women and priesthood during the period of the monarchy and later, then, is weighty and suggests that women did not exercise priestly functions in the Temple. The reason for their absence cannot be found in anything which is indigenous to Yahwism itself. Rather, it most likely stems from the Israelites' need to distinguish themselves from the orientation of their Canaanite neighbors. By limiting the priesthood to one sex, Israel tried to avoid the adoption of fertility rites into the legitimate worship of Yahweh.

The texts about Miriam come from writers belonging to the monarchical period and later. Hence, Miriam is not called a priestess and neither is her overall portrait in the texts clearly characterized as priestess. Indeed, apparently the writers had no such model available within legitimate Yahwism.

The above, however, does not necessarily bring to a close the question

---

[44]The Code of Hammurabi, for example, reflects various classes of priestesses. See G. R. Driver and J. C. Miles, *The Babylonian Laws* (2 vols.; Oxford: Clarendon, 1955 [vol. 1] 1952, 1960 [vol. 2]. See also Serge Sauneron, *The Priests of Ancient Egypt*, (New York: Grove, 1960) 67-69, and Blackman, "On the Position of Women in the Ancient Egyptian Hierarchy," 8-30.

[45]G. B. Gray, *Sacrifice in the Old Testament*, 192.

of whether or not the biblical portrait of Miriam *in some way* includes that of priestess. An attempt to answer the question is limited by the fact that little is known about Israel's early priesthood. According to Cody, priests in the early period were characterized by a connection with a sanctuary, specifically in the capacity of a consultor of oracles.[46]

The priestly role of consultor of oracles brings to mind the story of Num 12:2-9. Therein, Miriam is portrayed as one who claimed authority to speak God's word. Although this is not an ancient text, the fact is that the writer deemed it appropriate to cast Miriam as one of the protagonists in a controversy over oracular authority. I have suggested in chap 3 that in doing so, the writer of this narrative portrayed Miriam as representing the concerns of some of Israel's priests. The writer, then, appears to cast Miriam as belonging to Israel's priestly personnel.

Secondly, keeping in mind the picture of Miriam in Num 12:2-9 and Cody's description of early priests as consultors of oracles who were connected with a shrine, one might pursue the possibility of a priestly aspect to the portrait of Miriam by turning to the witness of Num 20:1b. If, as I shall argue in chap. 5, this text represents an early tradition which connected Miriam with Kadesh, and if von Rad is correct in viewing Kadesh as a sanctuary where divine decisions were rendered,[47] then here too a priestly characteristic to the Miriam portrait might be suggested.

Miriam's association with Aaron in the biblical traditions might be cited as another possible witness that her biblical portrait included elements of a priestly character. The designation of Miriam as Aaron's "sister" in Exod 15:20 appears to reflect a view that the prerogative of priestly activity lay in the cult. I have suggested above (p. 84) that it was precisely this early portrait of Miriam as a cultic leader which led Israel's late priestly family to claim Miriam as one of their own. In doing so the writer who added the "sister" designation to Exod 15:20 seems to have interpreted Miriam's role in the celebration as priestly in character. If this is correct it should be noted that this writer created a second

---

[46]Cody, *A History of Old Testament Priesthood*, 13. For a similar view of early Israelite priesthood, see A. S. Herbert, *Worship in Ancient Israel*, Ecumenical Studies in Worship, 5 (London: Butterworth 1959) 36ff. As is well known, this understanding of the role of Israel's early priests is not clearly distinguished from the role of some early prophetic figures in Israel's tradition. One might compare the role of the priest in Judges 17-18 with the portrait of Samuel, particularly as narrated in 1 Samuel 9-10.

[47]Von Rad, *Old Testament Theology* 1. 11-12.

anachronism to stand beside the "prophetess" designation which an earlier generation had added to the text.[48]

Because Miriam is never called a priestess and because the biblical writers did not cast her overall portrait on the model of a priestess, it would be incorrect to say that the biblical portrait of Miriam is captured by the designation "priestess" just as it is incorrect to say that Miriam's portrait in the texts is captured by the designation "prophetess" (see chap. 3). However, the possibility that at least some layers of Hebrew tradition interpreted her role as containing elements of a priestly character cannot be ruled out.

---

[48]The question of whether or not Miriam is characterized as a priestess cannot be answered on the basis of the genealogical texts which have been treated in this chapter. It has been shown that the specific purpose of both Numbers 26 and 1 Chronicles 5 was, in one way or another, to trace priestly lineage from Levi through Aaron. The genealogies branch off from a strictly linear pattern in the generations prior to those of Aaron's sons in order to present a more or less comprehensive list of the tradition's key figures in the pre-Aaronic and Aaronic generations. But Aaron was the decisive figure in the genealogies and the writer's purpose was focused upon him. To draw conclusions about a priestly role for Miriam, then, would be to find therein answers to questions which did not exist in the minds of the writers. Likewise, although in some texts (e.g., Ps 99:6) Moses is viewed as priest, one could not argue from the genealogical texts that Moses was a priest. In the genealogies Miriam and Moses were portrayed as belonging to post-exilic Israel's priestly family. This, however, does not indicate whether or not the genealogists witnessed to priestly roles for them.

5

The Three Remaining Texts

DEUTERONOMY 24:8-9

Of all the scriptural texts which mention Miriam, Deut 24:8-9 is perhaps the least helpful in an attempt to recover the content of the portrait of Miriam as that was passed down in Hebrew tradition. The text reads:

> Take heed, in an attack of leprosy, to be very careful to do according to all that the Levitical priests shall direct you; as I commanded them, so you shall be careful to do. Remember what the Lord your God did to Miriam on the way as you came forth out of Egypt.

The passage presupposes that the reader is acquainted with some established norms regarding the treatment of leprosy, although one cannot assume that the minute priestly legislation of Leviticus 13-14 was intended. Likewise, the text presupposes knowledge of Miriam and a tradition about her leprosy. Numbers 12 immediately comes to mind, although here too one cannot be certain that the latter text was known in its final form.

In the analysis which follows I shall seek to separate different literary strands reflected in this text. In addition, the question of content must be raised: what is the meaning of the text, and especially, what is the meaning of the reference to Miriam?

The Text and Its Origins

The injunction of Deut 24:8-9 appears in a collection of miscellaneous laws (Deut 23:15 - 25:19). The surrounding verses (Deut 24:6, 7, 10ff.) deal with the protection of the weak and one might conjecture that the injunction of Deut 24:8-9 reflects a concern for the humane treatment of lepers. However, since the wider context contains laws covering broad areas, it is difficult to be certain that there was a strict principle of organization which brought the passage about leprosy into its present context. Therefore I shall view the text apart from the section in which it appears.

Although Deut 24:8-9 was obviously intended as a directive to the community in handling cases of leprosy, it does not take the form of a legal prescription (cf. the conditional laws of Deut 21:15-17; 22:13-29; 24:1-4, 7; 25:1-3, 5-10, etc., and the apodictic laws of Deut 5:6-21; 15:1; 22:5, 9-11; 16:19, etc.). Rather, the style is exhortatory, a chief characteristic of Deuteronomic composition.[1] It falls within the stylistic pattern of the same school to illustrate and emphasize a particular directive by connecting it with an event in salvation history (as, e.g., in Deut 15:12-15; 16:1, 23:4-7; etc.). Hence, although the content rests upon older tradition (both the knowledge of existing practices regarding the treatment of lepers and familiarity with Miriam), literary features of the text indicate that it is a composition of the Deuteronomic school.

The text is marked by the use of both singular and plural forms of address and this phenomenon serves as a key for recognizing different literary strata within the passage.[2] If one sets aside the parts which appear in the plural, the text reads:

Take heed, in an attack of leprosy, to be very careful . . .
Remember what the Lord your God did to Miriam . . .

Taken together the singular parts form a complete and coherent thought.

---

[1] J. Blenkinsopp ("Deuteronomy," in *JBC*, ed. R. E. Brown, J. A. Fitzmyer and R. E. Murphy [Englewood Cliffs, New Jersey: Prentice-Hall, 1968], 116) writes: "The injunction to 'take care' introduces not a law but an exhortation typical of the Dt. sermon style (cf. 4:1, 9, 15; 8:11; 11:16; 12:32)." See also Wright, "The Book of Deuteronomy," in *IB* (1953) 2. 475.

[2] The alternation between singular and plural forms of address in the Book of Deuteronomy has long been noted and has served as a point of departure in separating *Urdeuteronomium* (characterized by the use of the singular) from later additions (characterized by the use of the plural). G. Minette de Tillesse ("Sections "tu" et sections "vous" dans le Deuteronome," *VT* 12 [1962] 29-87) assigns the plural additions to the Deuteronomic historian. For a survey of the research on this question, see E. W. Nicholson, *Deuteronomy and Tradition*, 22-34.

On the other hand, if one reads the plural parts by themselves (the directive to obey the Levitical priests in v 8 and "on the way as you came forth out of Egypt" in v 9), the same cannot be said. This leads me to view the singular text as having existed by itself at one time and the plural parts as editorial additions to the original text.[3] It is reasonable to regard the singular passage as belonging to *Urdeuteronomium* (seventh century B.C.) and the plural additions as the work of the Deuteronomic historian (sixth century B.C.).

Other evidence supports the suggestion that the plural passages belong to the Deuteronomic historian. G. Minette de Tillesse has noted that the use of the plural *haleᵂîyīm* (as opposed to the singular *halēᵂî*) is characteristic of plural passages of the Book of Deuteronomy and other works of the Deuteronomic historian.[4] In addition, the plural expression in v 9 ("on the way as you came forth out of Egypt") has exact parallels in Deut 23:5 and 25:17.[5] In all three cases (23:5, 24:9, 25:17), the plural expression occurs in otherwise singular passages. It bears the appearance, then, of a stylized expression stemming from a late redactor of *Urdeuteronomium*.

On the basis of this evidence, one can separate two literary strata in Deut 24:8-9. The original injunction read:

---

[3]Some commentators (e.g., von Rad, *Deuteronomy: A Commentary*, OTL [Philadelphia: Westminster, 1966] 151; Anthony Phillips, *Deuteronomy*, The Cambridge Bible Commentary [Cambridge: Cambridge University, 1973] 162; W. L. Moran, "Deuteronomy," in *A New Catholic Commentary on Holy Scripture*, ed. R. C. Fuller, L. Johnston and C. Kearns [Camden, New Jersey: Thomas Nelson and Sons, 1969] 272) view the reference to the Levitical priests as secondary. To my knowledge, no one has discussed the plural addition to Deut 24:9.

[4]DeTillesse ("Sections 'tu' et sections 'vous'," p. 81) also points out a theological difference. He says that, while the Levites have sacral functions in *Urdeuteronomium* (which de Tillesse connects with northern theology), they are not priests and priests are not Levites. On the other hand, in the works of the Deuteronomic historian (which de Tillesse connects with southern theology), the Levites share in the full priestly ministry.

[5]Deut 23:4-7 says that Israel shall not allow Ammonites and Moabites into the assembly because "they did not meet you with bread and water on the way when you came forth out of Egypt." In Deut 25:17 the phrase ("Remember what Amalek did to you on the way as you came forth out of Egypt") introduces the rationale behind the directive to destroy Amalek. Cf. Josh 5:4-5 and 1 Sam 15:2.

> Take heed, in an attack of leprosy, to be very careful . . .
> Remember what the Lord your God did to Miriam . . .

The Deuteronomic historian supplemented the original injunction by adding the reference to the Levitical priests in v 8 and by extending the reference to Miriam in v 9 to include "on the way as you came forth out of Egypt."

Content

At the outset it must be admitted that the exact intent of this passage is elusive. The text is best understood in light of the Numbers 12 narrative[6] and no doubt rests on the same tradition although it is not certain that the Deuteronomic writers knew Numbers 12 in the same form in which it presently appears in the Massoretic text. Assuming, however, that Deut 24:8-9 rests upon some stage of the Numbers 12 tradition, one must ask precisely what in the latter was intended by the cryptic reference "Remember what the Lord your God did to Miriam . . ." Driver[7] understands the admonition as pointing the reader not only to how Miriam was suddenly smitten with leprosy but also to the seriousness with which it was handled (cf. Num 12:10ff.). In agreement with Driver, Craigie[8] says that the reference is both to Miriam's leprosy and to the procedure of purification while Phillips[9] says that the text teaches that both the disease and its cure are under God's control.[10]

---

[6]Almost all commentators refer readers of Deut 24:8-9 to the Numbers 12 account.

[7]S. R. Driver, *A Critical and Exegetical Commentary on Deuteronomy*, ICC (Edinburgh: T. and T. Clark, 1895) 275.

[8]Peter C. Craigie, *The Book of Deuteronomy*, NICOT (Grand Rapids, Michigan: William B. Eerdmans, 1976) 308.

[9]Phillips, *Deuteronomy*, 162.

[10]Other commentators have taken a safer course in not venturing a specific elaboration of the reference at all. See Wright, "The Book of Deuteronomy," in *IB* (1953) 2. 475; von Rad, *Deuteronomy*, 151; J. A. Thompson, *Deuteronomy: An Introduction and Commentary*, Tyndale Old Testament Commentaries (London: Inter-Varsity, 1974) 246; G. Henton Davies, "Deuteronomy," in *PCB*, ed. M. Black and H. H. Rowley (New York: Thomas Nelson and Sons, 1963) 279. Cf. Blenkinsopp, "Deuteronomy" in *JBC*, 116, who regards this as reflecting a concern for preserving the purity of the holy war camp although he does not specifically connect this interpretation with the reference to Miriam.

These interpretations are, of course, attempts to fill in what Deut 24:8-9 does not explicitly say. In full awareness that any other interpretation will suffer from the same handicap, I wish to tentatively offer my own understanding of the text. It is my view that the best understanding of this difficult passage entails separating the meaning of the original injunction from that of the edited text which has been passed down from the hand of the Deuteronomic historian.

The original text of v 8 ("Take heed, in an attack of leprosy, to be very careful") presupposes that leprosy does and will occur within the community. The focus of the injunction is on v 9, i.e., on the treatment of leprous persons. Hence, the injunction to remember what God did to Miriam is not a warning but rather a reference to that event in the past which is to be regarded as normative for the treatment of leprous persons.[11] In other words, the writer of Urdeuteronomium advised: as God handled Miriam's leprosy, so you also should do.

In my opinion, this original injunction was significantly altered with the addition of the plural passages. First of all, the addition to obey the Levitical priests specifies the earlier injunction to "be very careful" and, in so doing, the admonition to act in accord with priestly directives has replaced v 9 as the focus of the passage.[12] According to the Deuteronomic historian, in order to know how to handle cases of leprosy one no longer turns to events from the past (what God did to Miriam) but to the Levitical priests. With the addition to v 8, then, the reference to what God did to Miriam (v 9) effectively lost both its place as the focus of the original injunction and its function as a norm for treating leprous persons.[13]

If this is so, then what is the meaning of v 9 in the final text? My answer is that it became a warning—and at the same time a supporting example—in relation to the addition to v 8. This interpretation rests on the Numbers 12 tradition—not of God's treatment of Miriam's leprosy

---

[11]Perhaps the practice of excluding leprous persons from the community is intended.

[12]Phillips (Deuteronomy, 162) writes: "An original injunction to be careful to avoid leprosy has, as the plural form of address indicates, been changed by the Deuteronomic historian into a caution to act in accordance with priestly regulations."

[13]Moran ("Deuteronomy," in NCCHS, 272) alludes to the awkward and seemingly purposeless reference to Miriam after the injunction to obey the Levitical priests: "The injunction to obey the Levites seems secondary; the reference to Miriam then becomes more meaningful."

(vv 10ff.) but of how she came to have leprosy in the first place (vv 1ff.). In chap. 3 I suggested that behind the Numbers 12 controversy lay a struggle for power within priestly circles. I suggested that Aaron and Miriam represented Aaronic priests and that Moses represented Levites in that struggle. The Levites are vindicated by the divine speech of vv 6-8 and by the fact that Miriam was struck with leprosy (vv 10ff.). If the redactor of Deut 24:8-9 knew and understood the Numbers 12 tradition in this way, then his admonition to obey Levitical priests is supported by recalling Miriam's mistake: remember what happened to one of our ancestors when she questioned the authority of the Levites (i.e., Moses).

Finally, what is the meaning of the Deuteronomic redactor's addition to v 9: "on the way as you came forth out of Egypt"? The addition appears to identify Miriam as belonging to the exodus community. However, the facts that (1) the only other tradition of Miriam's leprosy which is extant (Numbers 12) is firmly situated in the wilderness and (2) the same expression (Deut 23:5 and 25:17) is used to refer to events in the wilderness show that the addition to Deut 24:9 intended to connect Miriam with the wilderness period and not with the exodus. The appearance of a very similar expression[14] used in apposition to hamīdĕbār in Josh 5:4,5 further identifies the stylized expression ("on the way as you came forth out of Egypt") as a reference to the wilderness period. In general, however, it must be said that the addition of this expression does not alter the content of the edited text. Perhaps its only purpose is to help the reader to recall more precisely the tradition of Numbers 12 (cf. the efforts to further identify Miriam in Exod 15:20, i.e., the designation of her as "prophetess, sister of Aaron").

Conclusions

Deut 24:8-9 offers no new information to the present study of the biblical portrait of Miriam. I have suggested that the writer of *Urdeuteronomium* recalled what God did to Miriam (presumably some form of the tradition of Num 12:10ff.) as a norm for the treatment of leprous persons, while the Deuteronomic historian used the same cryptic reference to cite her rebellion (some form of the tradition of Num 12:1ff.) as a warning to obey Levitical priests. Both writers presuppose that Miriam was a familiar

---

[14]In Josh 5:4-5 the expression appears in the third person plural whereas in Deut 23:5, 24:9 and 25:17 it appears in the second person plural.

figure in need of no introduction and that the tradition of her leprosy was known. The end of v 9 shows that she was portrayed as belonging to the wilderness period.

MICAH 6:4

Noth has aptly pointed out the negligible role played by Moses in the Hebrew scriptures outside the Pentateuch and traditions emanating from it.[15] I begin my analysis of the appearance of Miriam in Mic 6:4 with this observation for three reasons: (1) It sets in bold relief the striking quality of this singular mention of Miriam in the prophetic works. If the neglect of the overtowering figure of the Pentateuch outside Pentateuchal traditions is surprising, then all the more so is the fact that Miriam is even mentioned at all outside the Pentateuch since she appears with such infrequency within the Pentateuch itself. (2) Awareness of this phenomenon in the written traditions with regard to Moses might help in understanding how a figure like Miriam, who at one time undoubtedly enjoyed some prominence in Hebrew circles, could come across as a relatively insignificant figure if one were to judge by the number of times she is mentioned in the texts which remain. While Moses enjoys center stage in some writings, in others he hardly appears. This, however, is not to say that he was forgotten. The case is similar with Miriam. The few texts which mention her suggest that much more about her circulated at one time, either in the oral tradition or in written traditions which were not included in the canon. She is not mentioned often, but neither was she forgotten. (3) Finally, with few exceptions, extra-Pentateuchal appearances of Moses are to be traced primarily to the Deuteronomic writer and the Chronicler's works (which are dependent upon the Deuteronomic history). This fact serves as a clue to my conclusion regarding the date and origin of Mic 6:4.

The Text, Form and Content of Mic 6:1-5

[1]Hear what the Lord says:
Arise, plead your case before the mountains,
and let the hills hear your voice.

[2]Hear, you mountains, the controversy of the Lord,
and you enduring foundations of the earth;

---

[15]Noth, *Pentateuchal Traditions*, 156ff.

for the Lord has a controversy with his people,
and he will contend with Israel.

[3]"O my people, what have I done to you?
In what have I wearied you? Answer me.

[4]For I brought you up from the land of Egypt,
and redeemed you from the house of bondage;
and I sent before you Moses, Aaron and Miriam.

[5]O my people, remember what Balak king of Moab devised,
and what Balaam the son of Beor answered him,
and what happened from Shittim to Gilgal,
that you may know the saving acts of the Lord."

The Hebrew text of this passage is relatively free of major difficulties.[16] Some commentators see problems with the line in v 4 which mentions Miriam. Smith[17] omits the entire line (4c) as a gloss while Mays[18]
transfers the ʿammî ("my people") which appears at the beginning of v 5 in
the MT to the end of v 4 and emends it to ʿimmō so that the line reads:

I sent Moses before you,
Aaron and Miriam with him.

Smith and Mays advance these suggestions (and propose other textual
changes) in the interest of preserving a balanced rhythm in the passage. In
the present study I shall treat the MT as it stands, especially since the
proposed changes in this case are not supported by the ancient versions.[19]

---

[16]For acceptable solutions to the few problems which the text does
have, see the suggestions in the textual apparatus of *BHK*.

[17]J. M. P. Smith, "Micah," in *A Critical and Exegetical Commentary on
Micah, Zephaniah, Nahum, Habakkuk, Obadiah and Joel*, ed. Smith, W. H.
Ward and J. A. Brewer, ICC (New York: Charles Scribner's Sons, 1911)
118-21.

[18]J. L. Mays, *Micah: A Commentary*, The OTL (Philadelphia:
Westminster, 1976) 128.

[19]See Leslie C. Allen (*The Books of Joel, Obadiah, Jonah and Micah*,
NICOT [Grand Rapids, Michigan: W. B. Eerdmans, 1976] 364) who points to
the preponderance of the 3 + 3 rhythm in the passage but adds: "Many
have succumbed to the temptation of using this major meter as a means
of bringing the rest into conformity, but the conjectural results reflect
little more than an exercise in versification." In staying with the MT, I am

Following a typical introduction to a prophetic oracle in 6:1a, the
singular imperative of 6:1b indicates that the prophet is called to engage
the community in a lawsuit (*rîb*) with the Lord.[20] V 2 summons the mountains and the foundations of the earth to witness the trial proceedings
which follow.[21] V 3 reflects the charge: Yahweh has been accused of fault
or negligence by the community.[22] In vv 4-5 the defendant's innocent plea
takes the form of a recital of Yahweh's saving acts on Israel's behalf.[23]

---

in agreement with J. T. Willis, "The Structure, Setting and Interrelationships of the Pericopes in the Book of Micah" (Ph.D. dissertation, Vanderbilt Divinity School, 1966), see p. 340, n. 1 of this work.

[20]On the *rîb* pattern, see especially B. Gemser, "The Rîb-Pattern in
Hebrew Mentality," in *Wisdom in Israel and in the Ancient Near East*, ed.
M. Noth and D. W. Thomas (Leiden: Brill, 1955) 120-37; H. B. Huffmon,
"The Covenant Lawsuit in the Prophets," *JBL* 78 (1959) 285-95; and J.
Limburg, "The Root ריב and the Prophetic Lawsuit Speeches," *JBL* 88
(1969) 291-304. I prescind from a discussion of whether or not the lawsuit
in Micah 6 is specifically covenantal in character since that distinction
seems to have no bearing on my conclusions about Miriam.

[21]On the interpretation of the reference to natural phenomenon here
see the discussion by P. Watson, "Form Criticism and an Exegesis of
Micah 6:1-8," *Restoration Quarterly* 7 (1963) 65-66.

[22]Watson ("Form Criticism and an Exegesis of Micah 6:1-8," p. 64) says
that ". . . Yahweh is taking them to court for libel, as it were."

[23]Many scholars regard v 5 as the end of the *rîb* unit, noting that the
Gattung changes to that of a torah entrance liturgy in vv 6-8. See, e.g.,
Westermann, *Basic Forms of Prophetic Speech*, 204; H. Gunkel, *The
Psalms: A Form-Critical Introduction*, (Philadelphia: Fortress [Facet
Books], 1967) 22; cf. Mays, *Micah: A Commentary*, 127ff. J. M. P. Smith
(*Micah*, 122) notes the abruptness of the change between 6:1-5 and 6:6-8
and posits that vv 1-5 comprise a fragment of what was originally a longer
address, while R. E. Wolfe ("The Book of Micah," in *IB* [1956] 6. 938) says
"The person who recorded it [the trial proceedings] apparently remembered only the first part of the proceedings." Willis ("The Structure of the
Book of Micah," *SEÅ* 34 [1969] 5-42) accounts for the abrupt change
between vv 1-5 and 6-8 by positing the unlikely situation that the community, suddenly moved to repentance, interrupts the prophet to inquire
what they can do to be forgiven their obvious ingratitude. According to
Willis, the prophet replies (v 8) that they already know the answer to their
question and resumes the lawsuit in vv 9-16. Gemser ("The Rîb-Pattern in
Hebrew Mentality," 130-31), Watson, ("Form Criticism and an Exegesis of
Micah 6:1-8," 61-72) and Huffmon ("The Covenant Lawsuit in the Prophets," 287) join Willis in seeing the lawsuit in Micah 6 as extending beyond
v 5.

Other recitals of Yahweh's saving acts are found in the so-called historical creeds, covenant texts, some prophetic judgment oracles and some lawsuit texts. In general, the content of these recitals characteristically corresponds to the basic confession of Israel, i.e., divine involvement in the nation's history. However, as studies have shown, the specific details of this involvement are rarely, if ever, expressed exactly alike in the recitals.[24]

The brief recital of Mic 6:4-5 recalls the bringing out of Egypt and the crossing of the Jordan in addition to Yahweh's saving acts in sending human intermediaries between the two events. The line of primary interest for the present study is v 4c. What does its content add to the biblical portrait of Miriam?

This question has not been the subject of lengthy discussion among scholars. Leslie Allen simply notes that Miriam appears here alongside Moses and Aaron. Allen reminds his readers that Miriam is the singer and "prophetess, sister of Aaron" of Exodus 15.[25] D. W. Thomas[26] and D. Ryan[27] remark that this is the only passage in prophetic literature which mentions Aaron and Miriam and Smith[28] notes that the prominence given in Mic 6:4 to Aaron and Miriam is not present in earlier sources.[29] Finally, Mays explains the text as follows:

> The use of all three names in the role of commissioned leaders in the wilderness may result from a reflection on the

[24]Von Rad, The Problem of the Hexateuch and Other Essays (New York: McGraw-Hill, 1966) 3ff.; Westermann, Basic Forms of Prophetic Speech, 182; and Mendenhall, "Covenant Forms in Israelite Tradition," in BAR (ed. E. F. Campbell, Jr., and D. N. Freedman; Garden City, New York: Doubleday and Co., 1970) 3. 32-33.

[25]Allen, The Books of Joel, Obadiah, Jonah and Micah, 367. Mays (Micah: A Commentary, 134) too says that the role assigned to Miriam here "may be an interpretation of Exod 15:20."

[26]D. Winton Thomas, "Micah," in PCB (ed. M. Black and H. H. Rowley; New York: Thomas Nelson and Sons, 1963) 633.

[27]D. Ryan, "Micah," in NCCHS (ed. R. C. Fuller, L. Johnston and C. Kearns; New York: Thomas Nelson and Sons, 1969) 712.

[28]J. M. P. Smith, Micah, 121.

[29]S. Goldman ("Micah," in The Twelve Prophets ed. A. Cohen;[London: Soncino Press, 1961] 179) reports the typically imaginative Targum interpretation of this text: " . . . Moses is to teach religion and the law, Aaron to show the way of atonement, and Miriam to instruct the women."

attribution of prophet to all three (Ex. 7:1; 15:20f.), which has
its point of departure in Hos. 12:13.[30]

My answer to the question of content of the biblical portrait of Miriam
as reflected in Mic 6:4 is threefold. First of all, the text confirms the
general picture of Miriam established in previous chapters of this study,
i.e., that Miriam is portrayed as having held a leadership position in
Israel's early history. Mic 6:4, however, is little help in attempting to
further specify that position. In fact, unlike the Pentateuchal texts, Micah
says nothing of Miriam's leadership in cult (Exod 15:20-21), of her role as
a prophetic figure (Exod 15:20), or of her kinship relationship to Moses and
Aaron (Num 26:59, 1 Chr 5:29).

Secondly, while the text in Micah does not specify Miriam's leadership
role, it does say that her being sent (together with Moses and Aaron) is
regarded as one of Yahweh's saving acts on behalf of the people of Israel.
No recollection of the divine judgment for Miriam's having confronted
Moses surfaces here (cf. Num 12:10ff.). What appears in Mic 6:4 is not
only the view that Miriam was fully endorsed as a leader in the early
Israelite community but also the view that she was divinely commissioned
as such.

Finally, this text (like Num 12:1-15, Num 20:1b and Deut 24:9) appears
to designate Miriam as specifically belonging to the period of the wilderness wanderings.[31] Four saving acts by Yahweh are recounted here: the
coming out of Egypt,[32] the appointment of leaders for the wilderness
journey,[33] the blessing by Balaam in spite of Balak's evil intent, and the
crossing of the Jordan.[34]

---

[30]Mays, *Micah: A Commentary*, 130.

[31]Although at first glance the addition to Deut 24:9 ("as you came
forth out of Egypt") seems to contradict this, see the analysis of this
addition in the previous section of this chapter.

[32]With regard to the coming out of Egypt, Mic 6:4, like many other
texts (e.g., Exod 20:2, Deut 6:21-23, 1 Sam 10:18, Jer 2:6, Amos 2:10, Ps
105:37, 43, etc.) attests that it was Yahweh alone who brought Israel out
of Egypt. Other extra-Pentateuchal texts which witness to the leadership
of Moses (Hos 12:14) or Moses and Aaron (Josh 24:5, 1 Sam 12:6-8, Ps
105:26, and probably Ps 77:21), however, explicitly place the leadership of
these two as prior to or contemporary with the exodus event.

[33]It is noteworthy that texts outside the Pentateuch which refer to
leadership in the wilderness generally witness to Yahweh's leadership
alone (see Jer 2:6, Amos 2:10, Ps 78:52, Ps 136:16, Neh 9:12). Mic 6:4, on
the other hand, refers to human leadership in the wilderness wanderings.

[34]Mays (*Micah: A Commentary*, 130) seems to agree in seeing four

In sum, the content of Mic 6:2-5, cast in the form of a lawsuit speech,
reflects a portrait of Miriam similar to that of the Pentateuch, i.e., that
she was regarded as a leader alongside Moses and Aaron and that the
exercise of her leadership took place during the period of the wilderness
wanderings. What is distinctive about the view of Miriam in Mic 6:4 is
that her leadership is explicitly regarded as having been divinely commissioned.

I turn now to the question of the date and origin of this passage. When
was it written and who preserved and transmitted this memory of Miriam?

The Date and Origin of Mic 6:2-5

There are elements in Mic 6:2-5 which indicate that the text does not
stem from the eighth century prophet.[35] First of all, passages in chaps. 1-
3, which can safely be regarded as coming from the eighth century prophet[36] are addressed to leaders in Jerusalem whereas 6:2-5 appears to be
directed to all Israel. The latter is clear at the end of v 2 ("for the Lord
has a controversy with his people and he will contend with Israel") and in
the addressees of vv 3 and 5 ("O my people"). Secondly, in chaps. 1-3
(eighth century) the addressees seem to lack no confidence regarding their
stance before Yahweh in spite of their unjust practices. On the other
hand, the lawsuit (especially in Mic 6:3) reflects a feeling on the part of
the community that it has been the object of Yahweh's (unjust) negligence
or punishment. The audience and content of Mic 6:2-5, then, suggest a
date of composition which is later than eighth century Judah. The situation more appropriately reflects the period of the exile.[37]

---

saving acts recounted here and in regarding v 4c as referring to leadership
in the wilderness.

[35] The fact that this text follows the *rîb* pattern is not especially
helpful in attempting to date the passage since that pattern is used by
prophets from Hosea to Malachi. See Mays, *Micah: A Commentary*, 129, n.
f, for examples.

[36] While there continues to be much scholarly debate over which sections of the Book of Micah belong to the eighth century prophet from
Moresheth and which are later additions, it is widely agreed that most of
chaps. 1-3 go back to Micah himself. See Knud Jeppeson, "New Aspects of
Micah Research," *JSOT* 8 (1978) 3-32.

[37] Mays, *Micah: A Commentary*, 130-31. Cf. Watson ("Form Criticism
and an Exegesis of Micah 6:1-8," p. 62, n. 9), who assumes that the passage is authentically Mican.

Furthermore, the language and style of Mic 6:2-5 indisputably point to a late period. Evidence for this has been detailed by Mays:

> The verb "ransom" (v. 4a) used for the exodus occurs in Deut. 7:8; 13:6; 9:26; 15:15; 21:8; 24:18; II Sam. 7:23 (deuteronomic historian); Neh 1:10; and the late Ps. 78:42. With "house of slaves" as an interpretative synonym for Egypt, the verb appears only in Deut. 7:8; 13:16. "House of slaves" is itself a favourite phrase of deuteronomic style (see Deut. 6:12; 8:14; 13:11); 5:6 = Ex. 20:2; Ex. 13:14; Josh. 24:17; Judg. 6:8 can be attributed to the same literary sphere; finally, Jer. 34:13. . . . The call to remember (v. 5a) connected with the motif of the saving history and used to enforce the relation to YHWH is a feature of deuteronomic paranesis (Deut. 5:15; 7:18; 8:2, 18; 9:7; 15:15; 16:3, 12; 24:9, 18, 22); 25:17 is a near parallel to v. 5a. The expression "in order to know" ($l^ema^can\ da^cat$) is found only in the deuteronomic history (Josh. 4:24; Judg. 3:2; I Kings 8:60) and Ezek. 38:16; note the similarity of use in Josh. 4:24; I Kings 8:60.[38]

Having said this, one must also note that there is nothing particularly late about the specific details of the brief historical recital of vv 4-5. First of all, the recital terminates with the crossing of the Jordan, recalling neither the conquest proper nor the plenitude of the land (cf. Josh 24:2-13, Jer 2:6-8, 1 Sam 12:6ff., etc.). Secondly, the mention of Balaam in 6:5a is clearly not the creation of the Deuteronomic writer but rather rests on the early (JE) story of Numbers 22-24. Likewise reference to the crossing of the Jordan as a movement "from Shittim to Gilgal" in 6:5b stems from the early epic traditions (Num 25:1, Josh 2:1, 3:1). Certainly the same is true of the mention of the coming out of Egypt in Mic 6:4, although the language in which that event is expressed is specifically Deuteronomic. Is the portrait of Miriam in Mic 6:4 a Deuteronomic innovation or does it too go back to early tradition? There is plenty of evidence to support the latter alternative. Miriam appears elsewhere in the Deuteronomic corpus in Deut 24:9, a text which presupposes familiarity with the tradition of Numbers 12.[39] The Deuteronomic redactor, then,

---

[38]Mays, *Micah: A Commentary*, 130.

[39]In addition, since he echoed the JE traditions about Balaam and the movement from Shittim to Gilgal, one can also suppose that the Deuteronomist knew the early tradition of Miriam's celebration (Exod 15:20-21).

had at his disposal the tradition that Miriam was a leading voice in the wilderness community.

The portrait of Miriam as a leader in the wilderness, then, was not an innovation on the part of the writer of Mic 6:4. The entire recital reflects knowledge of the older traditions. In addition, it would be unheard of in the context of a lawsuit proceeding to present as one of Yahweh's saving acts something that was entirely new to the community. Westermann has pointed out that, although the speaker/writer had a certain degree of freedom in formulating the details of such recitals, in the overall content he was limited to traditions which were part of the community's confession.[40] However, it is important to note that, although the Deuteronomic writer of Mic 6:4 probably echoed early tradition in representing Miriam as a leading figure in the wilderness community, he did add a new dimension—a profound affirmation—of this early portrait of Miriam by presenting her leadership as having been divinely commissioned.

Finally, a comparison of Mic 6:4 with a very similar Deuteronomic text, 1 Sam 12:7-8, indicates that Miriam was not automatically and universally a standard part of Israel's tradition but rather an active figure in the confession of a particular segment of Israel, namely the south. 1 Sam 12:6ff., like Mic 6:2-5, is a lawsuit text and its language and context (a negative appraisal of the establishment of the monarchy) bear clear indications that it too came from the hand of the Deuteronomist.[41] The lines of special concern for the present study are vv 7-8:

> Now therefore stand still, that I may plead with you before the Lord concerning all the saving deeds of the Lord which he performed for you and for your fathers. When Jacob went into Egypt and the Egyptians oppressed them, then your fathers cried to the Lord and the Lord sent Moses and Aaron, who brought forth your fathers out of Egypt, and made them dwell in this place.

The poignant difference between this text and Mic 6:4 is clear: 1 Samuel 12 names only Moses and Aaron as leaders whereas Mic 6:4 includes

---

[40]Westermann, *Basic Forms of Prophetic Speech*, 182.

[41]On 1 Samuel 12 as a Deuteronomic text, see. e.g., H. W. Hertzberg, *I and II Samuel: A Commentary* OTL (Philadelphia: Westminster, 1964) 96-97 and A. D. H. Mayes, "The Rise of the Israelite Monarchy," *ZAW* 90 (1978) 10-11; cf. the discussion by G. B. Caird, "The First and Second Books of Samuel," in *IB* (1953) 2. 941.

Miriam alongside them.[42] If both texts come from a Deuteronomic hand, how is this difference to be explained?

One possible explanation is the following. During the period of their activity, the Deuteronomic editors seem to have had access to a wealth of written traditions (e.g., historical writings but also prophetic works) which had been carried to Babylon by different segments of the exiled population. 1 Sam 12:7-8 bears an affinity to anti-monarchical views which were prominent in the north. On the other hand, the Mican corpus must have been preserved, transmitted and carried into exile by disciples of the prophet from the south. While it is true that the north and south, no doubt, shared a common confession regarding the broad outline of Yahweh's ancient saving acts (exodus, wilderness, conquest), the particular details of such confessions varied. Perhaps the tradition of Miriam as a leader in the wilderness community was one such detail of Yahweh's saving activity preserved especially in the south. This suggestion lends credence to Noth's view that the traditions about Miriam were preserved and transmitted in the south.[43]

In conclusion, an analysis of Mic 6:2-5 advances the pursuit of the biblical portrait of Miriam in the following ways: (1) The content of the text confirms the Pentateuchal tradition that Miriam was a leader alongside Moses and Aaron and that, in this role, she was portrayed as belonging to the wilderness period. (2) Although the writer of Mic 6:4 echoed early tradition in presenting Miriam as a leader in the wilderness, he added a new and weighty dimension to that early tradition of the biblical portrait of Miriam when he presented the leadership (like that of Moses and Aaron) as having been divinely commissioned. (3) The date of this passage shows that Miriam was an active figure in Israel's tradition during the sixth century when a Deuteronomic writer added the lawsuit of 6:2-5 to the Mican corpus. (4) Finally, the mention of Miriam in Mic 6:4

---

[42]R. E. Wolfe ("The Book of Micah," in *IB* [1956] 6. 936) has noted the similarity between the passage in Micah 6 and that of 1 Samuel 12 and has suggested that the former might be dependent upon the latter. He takes no cognizance of the difference between the two passages which I have noted.

[43]Noth (*Pentateuchal Traditions,* 182) bases his view on the southern provenance of the Miriam tradition on the prophetess designation in Exod 15:20, calling Miriam a "southern Judean colleague of Deborah" (cf. Judg 4:4). He also says that Miriam's close association with Aaron in the tradition points to a southern provenance.

supports the view that the preservation and transmission of her memory is
to be traced to southern circles of Hebrew tradition.

NUMBERS 20:1

Only one text which mentions Miriam remains to be treated, i.e., the
notice of her death and burial at Kadesh which appears in Num 20:1 near
the end of the wilderness narratives. The text reads as follows:

> And the people of Israel, the whole congregation, came into
> the wilderness of Zin in the first month, and the people
> stayed at Kadesh; and Miriam died there, and was buried
> there.[44]

It is commonly accepted opinion that different literary strata are
reflected in Num 20:1. This serves as the starting point of an analysis of
the text. In addition, I shall discuss the origin of the respective strata and
the reason for their combination. Finally, I shall examine the content of
Num 20:1b for its impact on a study of the biblical portrait of Miriam.

The Text and Its Origins

There is good reason for regarding the notice of Miriam's death and
burial at Kadesh as having originally circulated apart from the itinerary
of Num 20:1a. The initial clue is the change of subject from "the people of
Israel, the whole congregation" (v 1a) to simply "the people" (v 1b).[45]

---

[44]The text is secure except for the omission of the designation of the
year referred to by the phrase "in the first month." This is commonly
noted by commentators. The most probable explanation is that a late
editor has omitted the year designation in an effort to smooth over the
discrepancy between the JE tradition that the Israelites went straight
from Egypt to Kadesh (Num 13:26) and P's view that they arrived at
Kadesh only in the fortieth year (cf. Num 33:36-39). For a discussion of
the discrepancy, see de Vaux, *The Early History of Israel*, esp. pp. 419-25.

[45]The subjects used in itinerary texts are diverse. Implicitly, of course,
the subject is always Israel. Explicitly, this is variously specified as
"Israel" (Exod 19:2), "the people of Israel" (Exod 12:37a; Num 10:12; Num
21:10; Num 22:1), "all the congregation of the people of Israel" (Exod 16:1;
Exod 17:1), "the people of Israel, the whole congregation" (Num 20:1a, 22),
and "the people" (Num 11:35; Num 12:16; cf. Num 20:1b). For an analysis

Secondly, the verb of v 1a (bo⁾) occurs with some regularity in itinerary texts whereas the verb of v 1b (yašab) never occurs in wilderness itineraries. Finally, while the content of verse 1a is such that it must essentially be viewed as an itinerary text, the same cannot be said of verse 1b since the latter lacks information about departure, arrival, and journey. Num 20:1b even seems out of place as an expansion of the itinerary notice of v 1a, for material which might authentically be called additional information in itinerary texts characteristically elaborates upon the people (e.g. Exod 12:37, 13:18), the journey (Exod 17:1), the date of arrival or departure (Exod 16:1, 19:1f., cf. Num 20:1a), or else it describes the particular location, usually in geographical terms (Exod 13:17, 13:20, 16:1, 20:11; cf. Exod 15:27). Expansions in itinerary texts never refer to an event connected with the place.

The notice of Miriam's death and burial at Kadesh, then, must be viewed as a piece of information stemming from a different author than that of the itinerary of Num 20:1a with which it has been combined. The differences which mark the two parts of Num 20:1 point to different authors as do recent studies which show that itinerary texts bear linguistic and structural cohesiveness apart from the material with which they have been attached in the final text.[46]

A priestly hand seems to be evident in the (editorial?) reference to "the whole congregation" in Num 20:1a.[47] There is also evidence for suggesting that the juxtaposed notation of Miriam's death and burial is to be traced to a late editor for it can hardly be accidental that, in the final text, the deaths of the three wilderness leaders coincide with the last three stops on the wilderness journey. This probably explains why the notice of Miriam's death and burial has been appended to Num 20:1a and not to earlier references to Kadesh (e.g., Num 13:26ff.).

---

of the linguistic characteristics of itinerary texts see Coats, "The Wilderness Itinerary," CBQ 34 (1972) 135-52, esp. pp. 136-38.

[46]See Coats, "The Wilderness Itinerary," and Jerome T. Walsh, "From Egypt to Moab: A Source Critical Analysis of the Wilderness Itinerary," CBQ 39 (1977) 20-33.

[47]Num 20:1a is assigned to the priestly writer or editor by virtually all commentators. Note, however, the reluctance of recent studies (e.g., Coats, "The Wilderness Itinerary" and Walsh, "From Egypt to Moab") to assign the wilderness itineraries to any of the four standard narrative sources.

If vv la and lb of Numbers 20 were brought together by a late editor, this is not to say that the tradition of Miriam's death and burial at Kadesh is the creation of a late writer. A comparison with the death reports of Aaron and Moses supports this.

The death reports of Aaron (Num 20:22ff.) and Moses (Deuteronomy 34) are traced to P in the case of Aaron and to P and Dtr. in the case of Moses.[48] The reports bear similarity to one another. For example, both Aaron and Moses die on mountains, both are mourned for thirty days, both accounts mention successors in office. Aaron lacks a grave tradition and the location of Moses' grave is uncertain.[49] Moreover, a theological interest is clear when one notes that, on the one hand, the account of Aaron's death (Num 20:22ff.) follows neatly upon the P writer's account of why Aaron and Moses had to die in the wilderness (Num 20:10-13; cf. v 24) and, on the other hand, that the narrative preceding the account of Moses' death (Deut 32:48-52) recalls the same incident. When Num 20:1b is viewed alongside the death reports of Aaron and Moses, it is immediately clear that the notice of Miriam's death and burial lacks the literary and theological characteristics of priestly composition. One can legitimately conclude that the notice of the Num 20:1b came from an early source.[50]

The brevity of Num 20:1b and its lack of distinctive literary character-istics pose difficulties for assigning this text to either J or E. Scholars have based their views on other texts in which Miriam is mentioned. Hence, Gray says that the literary strand here is E and cites the mention of Miriam in Exod 15:20f. and Numbers 12 (which, he says, are E) as

---

[48]See, e.g., G. B. Gray, *Numbers*, 269-71; Noth, *Numbers*, 152-54 and *Pentateuchal Traditions*, 170-73, 178, 226; de Vaux, *The Early History of Israel*, 553; Snaith, *Leviticus and Numbers*, 278; and J. L. Mays, *The Book of Leviticus. The Book of Numbers*, The Layman's Bible Commentary (Richmond, Virginia: John Knox, 1963) 112.

[49]On the similarities of the two reports see Noth's discussion in *Pentateuchal Traditions*, 178 and in his *Numbers*, 153.

[50]The similarity between Num 20:1b and Deut 10:6 ("There Aaron died and there he was buried") probably indicates that the Deuteronomic writer had the notice of Num 20:1b available to him. Note that the priestly writer's location of Aaron's death at Mount Hor is irreconcilable with the witness of Deut 10:6 which says that he died at Moserah (probably to be identified with the Moseroth of Num 33:38, a station prior to the Israel-ites' arrival at Kadesh).

supporting evidence.[51] (Noth,[52] on the other hand, refers to the same texts as a basis for his view that the reference to Miriam's death and burial belong to J. Mays[53] assigns Num 20:1b to JE.

The difficulty of linking the mention of Miriam in Exod 15:20f. and Numbers 12 to either J or E exclusively and the absence of distinguishing characteristics in the brief notation of Miriam's death in Num 20:1b prevent us from determining the literary source of the latter on linguistic grounds. Because Kadesh seems to be more prominent in the J source than in E,[54] Num 20:1b might tentatively be regarded as belonging to J. This possibility is strengthened if the tradition about Miriam recorded in Mic 6:4 likewise had a southern provenance (see above, p. 115).

The foregoing analysis of Num 20:1 shows (1) that the notice of Miriam's death and burial at Kadesh (v 1b) has been secondarily attached to the itinerary of v 1a, (2) that it lacks the literary and theological characteristics of the P writer's accounts of the deaths of the other wilderness leaders, and therefore (3) that its origin is to be sought in an early source, possibly J. While a certain editorial logic can be seen in the fact that the notice of Miriam's death lies in close proximity to the story of the sin which brought Moses and Aaron's deaths (Num 20:2-13) and the subsequent account of Aaron's death (Num 20:22ff.), it is noteworthy that the early notice of Miriam's death seems not to have been altered in any way when a later editor placed it in Numbers 20. In other words, taken by itself Numbers 20:1b shows no signs of having been constructed to fit any literary or theological schema. Rather, it "presumably reproduces a tradition that knew of a grave of Miriam in Kadesh."[55]

Num 20:1 and the Biblical Portrait of Miriam

Num 20:1 contributes several important considerations to a study of the biblical portrait of Miriam.

---

[51] G. B. Gray, *Numbers*, 98-99, 260. This writer (p. 206) also cites the likeness of the phraseology in Num 20:1b to that of Deut 10:6 which, he says, is an E tradition.

[52] *Numbers*, 145. In an earlier work the same writer had regarded the reference to Miriam in Numbers 20 as belonging to the P source. See *Pentateuchal Traditions*, 182-83.

[53] *The Book of Numbers*, 108.

[54] See de Vaux *The Early History of Israel*, 422.

[55] Noth, *Numbers*, 145.

First of all, the fact that Miriam's death and burial were recorded at all is striking. Whereas other figures in the wilderness community (Hur, Eldad and Medad, Moses' wife and father-in-law, etc.) disappeared without mention, the notice of Num 20:1b seems to be at least an implicit witness that Miriam was a figure of some significance whose memory was valued in Israelite tradition.

Secondly, the notice of Num 20:1b has all the appearances of being both an early and an authentic tradition. It is noteworthy that Miriam is the only member of the wilderness community whose death is recorded without being explicitly connected with divine punishment (cf. Num 20:2-13, 22ff.; 16; Deut 32:48-52).

Thirdly, in placing this early notice of Miriam's death and burial in Numbers 20 (instead of with another reference to Kadesh) a late writer (editor) implicitly contributes to the tradition that Miriam was a leader of some import in the wilderness community. It can hardly be accidental that, in the texts as they now stand, the deaths of Miriam, Aaron and Moses coincide with the last three stops on the wilderness journey.

Finally, Martin Noth has written that "a grave tradition usually gives the most reliable indication of the original provenance of a particular figure of tradition."[56] If this is true (and, to my knowedge it has not been refuted in recent scholarship), then the notice which appears in Num 20:1b most likely indicates that the Hebrew tradition about Miriam had its starting point at Kadesh.[57] At the very least, it can be said that early (and probably authentic) tradition firmly linked Miriam with Kadesh, an important shrine for the wilderness generation of Israelites.

---

[56]Noth, *Pentateuchal Traditions,* 169-70.

[57]This particular point will be important in chap. 6 where I offer an hypothesis regarding the historical starting point for the biblical portrait of Miriam.

6
Conclusions

The foregoing analysis of the seven texts which mention Miriam has been a necessary preparation for reaching the goal of this study. The task which remains is to synthesize the results of my study of the individual textual witnesses about Miriam so as to arrive at a characterization of her overall biblical portrait. This is the primary purpose of the present chapter. Secondarily, I shall offer an hypothesis about the possible historical starting point for Miriam's biblical portrait, a review of the various stages of development of Miriam's portrait in the biblical tradition, and some implications of my study.

THE BIBLICAL PORTRAIT OF MIRIAM

There can be no question about the chief characteristic of the biblical portrait of Miriam. Six of the seven (cf. Deut 24:9) texts which mention her represent her as a leader. In her initial appearance in the narratives (Exod 15:20-21) Miriam officiates at a celebration of the foundational event of Hebrew religion. In Numbers 12 she participates in what is ostensibly a crisis of leadership in the wilderness community. In designating Miriam as "sister" of Aaron (Exod 15:20) and of Aaron and Moses (Num 26:59; 1 Chr 5:29), the biblical writers use kinship terminology to express Miriam's parallel status in religious leadership vis-à-vis that of the two other leading figures in the wilderness. The three leaders also appear side by side in Mic 6:4. This text goes one step beyond the others by saying that Miriam (along with Moses and Aaron) was divinely commissioned as a leader in the wilderness. Finally, in placing the notice of Miriam's death and burial in Num 20:1, a late writer implicitly witnesses to Miriam's leadership position insofar as the deaths of the three wilderness leaders are artificially arranged so as to coincide with the last three stops on the wilderness journey.

Simply stated, then, the primary and most consistent element in the portrait of Miriam which is yielded by the texts is that she was a leader in the Hebrew community. Designating the specific character of her leadership position, however, is more difficult.

Can the overall portrait of Miriam be characterized as that of "prophetess"? In support of this, one might point to Exod 15:20 where Miriam is called a prophetess and to Num 12:2-9 where she is represented as one who claimed authority as a mediator of God's word. However, my study of these texts shows that the best understanding of the "prophetess" designation in Exod 15:20 is to regard it as an anachronism. Miriam is never represented as doing anything which is characteristically prophetic. Furthermore, my position is that in the controversy of Num 12:2-9, when Miriam claims authority as a mediator of God's word, she does so as a representative of a priestly, not a prophetic, group. Hence, the texts do not firmly present Miriam's portrait as that of "prophetess."

Might one say that in the figure of Miriam the tradition presents a priestess from Israel's early history? Here too the biblical witness is less than firm. In favor of such a designation, one might cite her leadership in the cult (Exod 15:20-21), the fact that she represents priests in the controversy of Num 12:2ff., and the strong witness of her association with Aaron (Exod 15:20; Num 26:59; 1 Chr 5:29). However, because leadership in Israel's early cult was not limited to priests, because Miriam is not called a priestess, and indeed because one cannot be certain that legitimate Yahwism ever allowed priestesses, the designation of Miriam as "priestess" does not seem warranted.

Regarding the sphere of Miriam's leadership activity, therefore, it seems most true to the texts to simply admit that the biblical portrait of Miriam does not reflect a clearly-differentiated role. One cannot adequately describe her by the use of a single title. What can be said with certainty is that the biblical writers did not artificially construct her overall portrait according to some model which they had in mind before handing on the traditions about her.

To say this, however, is not to exhaust the possibilities of what can be said about the Bible's presentation of Miriam's leadership. The texts portray Miriam as exercising leadership in two spheres.

The first of these is Israel's cult. Primary among those texts which represent Miriam as a cult official is Exod 15:20-21. I have suggested that the actions attributed to Miriam in Exod 15:20-21 are not mere expressions of joy but rather ritual action proper, i.e., her actions were intended as symbolic representations of the divine victory itself. I have also suggested that it was precisely the cultic nature of her activity in Exod

15:20-21 which led a subsequent writer to designate Miriam as "sister" of Aaron, the figurehead for late cult officials. Miriam's leadership in cult also accounts for her appearance in the Levitical genealogies of Num 26:59 and 1 Chr 5:29. In these texts Miriam is portrayed as belonging to the ancient Israelite family whose special authority and activity lay in cult leadership. Finally, it should be noted that Miriam's punishment in Num 12:10ff. was regarded, at least in the final stratum of composition, as ritual uncleanness.

In addition to being represented as a leader in cult, Miriam is firmly portrayed as a mediator of God's word. Num 12:2ff. makes this clear. The story does not deny her claim. It shows only that, as officials in announcing God's word, Miriam and Aaron were subordinate to Moses.

The biblical portrait of Miriam, then, represents her as a leader and the texts connect her leadership with the cult and with the announcing of God's word.[1] One might look to other early figures whose roles included both cultic activity and the mediation of God's word (e.g., Samuel,

---

[1] It is possible that, at some stage of tradition which has been lost, the two aspects of Miriam's leadership activity coalesced in a single position and that the generations who passed on the traditions about this figure did so under the influence of the gradual development of Israelite institutions which differentiated spheres of religious leadership. Israel's priesthood eventually came to be linked primarily with the prayers and sacrifices of the cult. The mediating of God's word then fell primarily within the realm of prophetic activity. As a result the emerging biblical tradition might have had difficulty in capturing Miriam's dual-faceted role under a single title. On the one hand, the texts which highlight her authority as a mediator of the divine will and call her a prophetess sought to reflect one aspect of her role. On the other hand, the ritual in honor of the Divine Warrior and her other connections with the cult and its personnel were biblical attempts to reflect Miriam's cultic office.

In the two longest texts which feature Miriam one might see attempts to bring the two aspects of her portrait together. On the surface of things the "prophetess" designation does not seem to have a direct relationship to Miriam's cultic leadership to which it is juxtaposed (Exod 15:20-21). However, if one views this as the biblical writer's attempt to capture both aspects of the figure of Miriam (her mediation of the divine word and her cult leadership), the juxtaposition is easier to understand. Likewise, the controversy over authority as a mediator of the divine word does not, at first glance, logically result in a punishment of ritual uncleanness (Numbers 12). However, it might well be that here too the biblical writers have reflected both aspects of what was, at some stage of tradition, a single office for Miriam.

Abiathar, and the Levite of Judges 17-18) for possible analogies to the biblical portrait of Miriam. However, strictly speaking, the texts about Miriam lack evidence that she had the authentic prophetic qualities which appear in the figure of Samuel just as the chief witness to Miriam's place in Israel's worship (Exod 15:20-21) lacks the oracular activity which was characteristic of early priests like Abiathar and the Levite of Judges 17-18. In addition, because in Exod 15:20-21 Miriam voices the worshippers' response to God's saving act instead of delivering God's word to the worshippers, one cannot characterize Miriam as a cult prophetess.

The dual aspect of Miriam's role might help to explain the textual witness of her position vis-à-vis Moses and Aaron. The biblical writers used kinship terminology to say that they regarded Miriam as a "colleague" of the other two religious leaders. The brothers-sister relationship denotes parallel status in the religious sphere. It is possible that generations of biblical writers, influenced by emerging religious institutions with differentiated leadership roles, felt a need to clarify Miriam's authority in the wilderness community vis-à-vis the emerging roles of the two other leader figures. Moses gradually assumed the role of mediator *par excellence* of the divine word. Hence, when the sphere of religious leadership was specified as that of mediating the divine word, Miriam and Aaron took subsidiary roles (Numbers 12). Aaron, on the other hand, gradually assumed the role of cult official *par excellence*. Hence, in this sphere Miriam and Moses took subsidiary roles (Num 26:59, 1 Chr 5:29). When authority in one or the other spheres of activity is not at stake, the wilderness leaders are simply presented alongside one another (Mic 6:4).

To summarize the above, it can be said that the primary characteristic of the biblical portrait of Miriam is that she was a leader in the wilderness. In addition, it can be said that, although the texts do not yield a single role designation of her leadership position, they do firmly reflect traditions which regarded Miriam as a cult official and as a mediator of God's word.

THE HISTORICAL MIRIAM?

Noth has written that "lacking any other plausible derivation, it is highly probable that behind the figure of Miriam stands a historical person."[2] While a "quest for the historical Miriam" has not been the goal of the present study, it is not irrelevant to make a suggestion here regarding

---

[2]Noth, *History of Pentateuchal Traditions*, 182.

an historical person who may have been the starting point for the biblical figure. The following, then, is offered as an hypothesis, supported by biblical data but ultimately incapable of being proven.

My analysis of Num 20:1b supports the view that this notice represents an early and authentic tradition that Miriam died and was buried at Kadesh. In chap. 5 I referred to Noth's view that "a grave tradition usually gives the most reliable indication of the original provenance of a particular figure of tradition."[3] If the grave tradition of Num 20:1b is authentic, and if Noth is correct in the view cited above, then one can legitimately posit that the biblical portrait of Miriam had its starting point in an historical person who was connected with the shrine at Kadesh.

Furthermore, one can explore the possibility that Miriam, at home in Kadesh, never left there, i.e., that she came to be associated with the Hebrew wanderers only upon their arrival at Kadesh. This view gains credence when one notes that Miriam's connections with other stations in the wilderness are tenuous.

Miriam's first appearance in the texts (Exod 15:20-21) is logically placed between the narrative account(s) of the Sea event (Exodus 14) and the community's departure from the Sea (Exod 15:22). However, the text reflects a cultic re-enactment of Yahweh's victory. That is to say, Miriam's dance and song in Exod 15:20-21 reflect stylized celebrations of Israel's Divine Warrior and this reduces the likelihood that her celebration took place historically on the shores of the Sea. The text's origin is better sought at one of the community's shrines. If the *Sitz im Leben* of Exod 15:20-21 is to be found in a liturgical event at a shrine, then it is permissible to view the witness of this text apart from its present literary context. If indeed Miriam did lead an early celebration of Yahweh's victory over the Egyptians (and there seems to be no other reason to account for the attribution of this celebration to Miriam), and if Kadesh was a major shrine along the wilderness route, one can posit that the celebration which Miriam led took place at Kadesh.

Secondly, the itinerary texts of Num 11:35 and Num 12:16 situate Miriam's controversy with Moses (Num 12:1-15) at Hazeroth. However, there is nothing in the narrative which ties the incident closely to this particular station in the wilderness. Rather, it is a controversy which might have been arbitrarily placed anywhere along the journey (cf. the controversies which also function as aetiologies, e.g., Exod 15:22ff.; Exod

---

[3]In chap. 5, see p. 120.

17:1-7; Num 11:4-34). The text, then, does not firmly associate Miriam
with Hazeroth.

Thirdly, other texts which bear reference to Miriam's place in the
tradition connect her only with the wilderness. Mic 6:4 refers to Miriam's
leadership in the wilderness. Likewise, my analysis (see chap. 5) of the
addition to Deut 24:9 ("Remember what the Lord did to Miriam *on the
way as you came forth out of Egypt*") shows that this too is a reference to
the wilderness period.

Num 20:1b, on the other hand, firmly situates Miriam at Kadesh and
this appears to be an authentic tradition.

Hence, the biblical texts portray Miriam as belonging to the wilderness
period and, within that, she is firmly connected only with Israel's stay at
Kadesh. This supports the possibility that the historical Miriam neither led
nor accompanied the Hebrews on their wilderness journey.

If the Hebrew wanderers first met Miriam at Kadesh, what was it about
her which led tradition to present her as it did, i.e., as a leader, as a cult
official and as a mediator of God's word? The most plausible explanation
seems to be that at Kadesh the wanderers encountered in Miriam an
already-established leader of the cult of that shrine.[4]

Von Rad writes that "Kadesh was . . . a well-known sanctuary where
divine justice was administered and cases in dispute decided."[5] In support

---

[4]In 1948, C. A. Simpson (*The Early Traditions of Israel: A Critical
Analysis of the Pre-Deuteronomic Narrative of the Hexateuch* [Oxford:
Basil Blackwell, 1948] 430) suggested that Miriam was an official (perhaps
a priestess) of the pre-Yahwistic cult at Kadesh which the Hebrews
encountered on their wilderness journey. Although Simpson proposed this
without substantiation or elaboration, my study brings me to similar
conclusions, with one exception. It can no longer be known whether
Miriam represented a pre-Yahwistic religion or traveled to Kadesh with
some other Yahwists who came there prior to the exodus group.

[5]*Old Testament Theology*, 1. 12. There is no scholarly agreement
regarding what can be posited with some reliability about Kadesh. On the
one extreme, Noth, (*Pentateuchal Traditions*, 164) writes that the Bible
has no such thing as a "Kadesh tradition" and "even less a tradition about
a cult of Kadesh." At the other extreme are scholars who hold that major
elements in Hebrew tradition (e.g., the Decalogue, cultic recital of the
law, sacrificial cult, Israel's social organization, and particularly their
method of administering justice) originated at Kadesh (see, e.g., W.
Beyerlin, *Origins and History of the Oldest Sinaitic Traditions*, [Oxford:
Basil Blackwell, 1965] 145-51 and sources cited therein). In following von
Rad, I have chosen a moderate view.

of this, one should note the designation of Kadesh as "Spring of Judgment" (Gen 14:7) and its connections with Massah ("testing"), Meribah, ("legal dispute"), and probably Marah ("bitterness").[6] It is plausible, then, to suggest that a "cult of judgment" was an important aspect of the Kadesh religion.[7] Such a heritage may have offered the Hebrews a religious thematization for the experience of "testing and being tested" in their relationship with Yahweh throughout the wilderness journey.

But does the biblical portrait of Miriam in any way warrant a connection between her and the "cult of judgment" at Kadesh? Perhaps the clearest link is Miriam's involvement in the struggle of Numbers 12 which deals specifically with the question of who speaks Yahweh's word (see the questions of Num 12:2 and the divine pronouncement of Num 12:6-8). If Numbers 12 reflects a dispute within priestly circles, as I have suggested, then presumably the controversy was over who speaks Yahweh's word in the cultic situation. Numbers 12, then, might well reflect an ancient memory of Miriam's role in voicing divine decisions in the cult of Kadesh.[8]

Other evidence for connecting Miriam with cultic judgment is not so easily found. It is tempting to point to Exod 15:20f. although it would be difficult to prove that Yahweh's victory at the Sea was specifically conceived as Yahweh's "judgment" on the Pharaoh. One might also note Miriam's inclusion in the Levitical genealogies and the Levites' connection

---

[6]The "bitter waters" incident at Marah (Exod 15:22ff.) makes one think of the "bitter waters" ordeals utilized in rendering juridical decisions (see especially Num 5:11-31 and Exod 32:20). Von Rad (Old Testament Theology, 1. 11-12) says that Massah and Meribah are probably to be understood as oases in the district of Kadesh. Num 20:2ff. identifies Kadesh with Meribah. The same identification appears in the name Meribath-Kadesh (Num 27:14; Deut 32:51; Ezek 47:19; Ezek 48:28). On the relationship of Marah, Massah, Meribah and Kadesh traditions, see Coats, Rebellion in the Wilderness, 47-82.

[7]On the judgment cult in Hebrew tradition, see J. F. X. Sheehan, "The Pre-P Narrative: A Children's Recital?" in Scripture in History and Theology: Essays in Honor of J. Coert Rylaarsdam (ed. A. L. Merrill and T. W. Overholt; Pittsburgh: Pickwick, 1977) esp. pp. 27-29 and sources cited therein.

[8]Although the final text of Numbers 12 is, of course, late, Simpson (The Early Traditions of Israel, 430) has suggested that the confrontation there might reflect ancient memories of an antagonism between Kadesh authorities (represented by Miriam) and the leader of the exodus group (Moses).

with the Kadesh oases. It was there that Levi was awarded the *urim* and *thummim,* ancient methods of rendering cultic decisions (Deut 33:8ff.).

Admittedly, evidence in the texts which mention Miriam rests too far under the surface to offer an indefensible argument that the Kadesh cult which she represented was specifically a judgment cult. However, Num 20:1b does firmly link Miriam with Kadesh just as Exod 15:20, the priestly controversy of Numbers 12, and the priestly genealogies of Numbers 26 and 1 Chronicles 5 firmly link her with cultic leadership. Several other texts link Kadesh with the cultic administration of divine justice. Taken together, these texts suggest that she was a leader in a judgment cult although this cannot be proved beyond quesiton. If indeed this was the case, it would have been a small step for the Hebrew wanderers to endorse as their own one whose tradition offered a thematization of the religious dimension of their journey (testing and being tested).

The Hebrew wanderers brought with them, however, not only memory of the struggles of life in the wilderness. They also brought memory of Yahweh's victory at the Sea. It is likely that this event was celebrated liturgically during their stay at the shrine at Kadesh. Miriam, an official at that shrine who had been endorsed by them, was remembered by the tradition as having led that celebration.

The preceding pages can be summarized as follows: the biblical portrait of Miriam as a leader who functioned as a cult official and as a mediator of God's word may have had roots in the memory of an historical person who officiated as a mediator of the divine will in the cult of Kadesh. It may have been there that the Hebrew wanderers met her and endorsed her as one of their own. This hypothesis helps to explain the absence of a biblical account of Miriam's rise to a leading position in the wilderness community and the biblical witness that she exercised leadership specifically in the cult and as an announcer of God's word.

STAGES IN THE DEVELOPING PORTRAIT

The biblical portrait of Miriam was not, of course, the work of one writer nor was it fully developed in a single era. It is possible to trace only in general outline the origins of the various pieces of the portrait.

The starting point for the biblical portrait, I suggest, is the notice of Miriam's death and burial at Kadesh. Miriam's celebration of Yahweh's victory is also early, although it reflects the more or less stereotyped features of other celebrations of Yahweh's victories. Likewise, the cryptic reference to the dispute over Moses' Cushite wife (Num 12:1) together with some form of the story of Miriam's leprosy (Num 12:10ff.) seem to belong to an early period.

The designation of Miriam as prophetess in Exod 15:20 probably stems from a redaction of that text.

The mention of Miriam in *Urdeuteronomium* (the singular parts of Deut 24:8-9) presupposes knowledge of Miriam, her leprosy and its treatment by Yahweh. A later redaction of this text (the plural additions to Deut 24:8-9) presupposes that the dispute over oracular authority (Num 12:2ff.) had been attached to the controversy over the Cushite wife and the story of Miriam's punishment (Num 12:1, 10ff.).

Miriam is pictured as a divinely-commissioned wilderness leader in the *Heilsgeschichte* recital of Mic 6:2-5. Although the text bears marks of Deuteronomic composition, the conservative nature of the confessional *Heilsgeschichte* within the lawsuit form cautions one against viewing the idea it contains as a late one. The writer of Mic 6:4 added new affirmation to an old tradition when he presented Miriam's leadership as divinely commissioned.

Miriam received considerable attention from the priestly circle of writers as they reworked the old Pentateuchal traditions. To these writers I attribute the designation of Miriam as Aaron's sister (Exod 15:20) and her presence in the Levitical family (Num 26:59). In addition, it was probably a priestly editor who appended the early notice of Miriam's death and burial at Kadesh (Num 20:1b) to the itinerary of Num 20:1a.

The latest mention of Miriam appears in 1 Chr 5:29. I have shown that the writer of this text was not simply copying a Pentateuchal text but rather that, like the genealogist of Num 26:59, he made a conscious decision in including Miriam in his genealogy. This indicates that Miriam remained an active figure in Israel's tradition until the latest periods of Hebrew canonical composition.

The seven texts which mention Miriam, then, span the entire period of canonical composition. From earliest times until the latest, biblical writers included her as a figure from their ancient past whose memory was valued. The very tenacity of the tradition of Miriam as a leader in the wilderness community might be cited as Israel's answer to a question Miriam herself is said to have voiced: "Has the Lord indeed spoken only through Moses?"

IMPLICATIONS OF THIS STUDY

The present work contributes to biblical scholarship and to theological reflection in the following ways.

First of all, in the introductory chapter I cited Martin Noth's pessimism regarding the possibility of saying anything at all about the biblical figure of Miriam. The present study, I think, supports the view that Noth's opinion was formed prematurely.

Secondly, until now both scholarly and popular writers have described Miriam most frequently as "prophetess" and "sister of Moses and Aaron." This study shows that, if writers are to continue to use these descriptions of Miriam, some significant qualifications are in order. It must be admitted that, although Miriam is called a prophetess, the biblical texts yield little basis for understanding her portrait in light of the roles of other prophetic figures. Likewise, the description of Miriam as "sister of Moses and Aaron" must be understood as part of a larger witness to Miriam's leadership in the wilderness community.

Finally, readers who wrestle with contemporary questions about leadership in the community of believers might well reflect on the biblical portrait of Miriam. Especially pertinent are Miriam's question (Num 12:2) and her punishment (Num 12:10ff.). The latter, it seems, is best viewed within the larger context of the Bible's affirmation of Miriam's place in Hebrew tradition.

Bibliography

WORKS OF REFERENCE CITED

Brown, F.; Driver, S. R. and Briggs, C. A. *A Hebrew and English Lexicon of the Old Testament, with an Appendix Containing the Biblical Aramaic, Based on the Lexicon of William Gesenius as Translated by Edward Robinson.* Rev. ed. Oxford: Clarendon Press, 1972.

Cowley, A. E. ed. *Gesenius' Hebrew Grammar.* Ed. and enl. E. Kautzsch. 2nd English ed. Oxford: Clarendon Press, 1910.

Gordon, C. H. *Ugaritic Manual.* Analecta Orientalia, 35. Rome: Pontifical Biblical Institute. 1955.

Kittel, R., ed. *Biblia Hebraica.* Stuttgart: Privileg. Württembergische Bibelanstalt, 1937.

May, H. G. and B. M. Metzger, eds. *The New Oxford Annotated Bible with the Apocrypha.* 2nd ed. New York: Oxford University Press, 1977.

COMMENTARIES CITED

Allen, L. C. *The Books of Joel, Obadiah, Jonah and Micah.* The New International Commentary on the Old Testament. Grand Rapids, Michigan: William B. Eerdmanns, 1976.

Blenkinsopp, J. "Deuteronomy." In *The Jerome Biblical Commentary,* pp. 101-22. Ed. R. E. Brown, J. A. Fitzmyer and R. E. Murphy. Englewood Cliffs, New Jersey: Prentice-Hall, 1968.

Bowman, R. A. "The Book of Ezra and the Book of Nehemiah." In *The Interpreter's Bible,* vol. III, pp. 551-819. Ed. G. A. Buttrick, et al. New York: Abingdon Press, 1954.

Caird, G. B. "The First and Second Books of Samuel." In *The Interpreter's Bible,* vol. II, pp. 855-1176. Ed. G. A. Buttrick, et. al. New York: Abingdon Press, 1953.

Clements, R. E. *Exodus*. The Cambridge Commentary. Cambridge: Cambridge University Press, 1972.

Coggins, R. J. *The First and Second Books of the Chronicles*. The Cambridge Bible Commentary. Cambridge: Cambridge University Press, 1976.

Craigie, P. C. *The Book of Deuteronomy*. The New International Commentary on the Old Testament. Grand Rapids, Michigan: William B. Eerdmans, 1976.

Curtis, E. L. and Madsen, A. A. *A Critical and Exegetical Commentary on the Books of Chronicles*. The International Critical Commentary. Edinburgh: T. and T. Clark, 1910.

Davies, G. H. "Deuteronomy." In *Peake's Commentary on the Bible,* pp. 269-84. Ed. M. Black and H. H. Rowley. New York: Thomas Nelson and Sons, 1963.

Elmslie, W. A. L. "The First and Second Books of Chronicles." In *The Interpreter's Bible,* vol. III, pp. 341-548. Ed. G. A. Buttrick, et. al. New York: Abingdon Press, 1954.

Driver, S. R. *A Critical and Exegetical Commentary on Deuteronomy*. The International Critical Commentary. Edinburgh: T. and T. Clark, 1895.

Goldman, S. "Micah." In *The Twelve Prophets,* pp. 153-89. Ed. A. Cohen. London: Soncino Press, 1961.

Gray, G. B. *A Critical and Exegetical Commentary on Numbers*. The International Critical Commentary. New York: Charles Scribner's Sons, 1906.

Gray, J. *I and II Kings*. 2nd ed. The Old Testament Library. Philadelphia: Westminster Press, 1970.

Herbert, A. S. *The Book of the Prophet Isaiah: Chapters I-XXXIX*. The Cambridge Bible Commentary. Cambridge: Cambridge University Press, 1973.

Hertzberg, H. W. *I and II Samuel: A Commentary*. Trans. J. S. Bowden. The Old Testament Library. Philadelphia: Westminster Press, 1964.

Hyatt, J. P. *A Commentary on Exodus*. The New Century Bible. London: Marshall, Morgan and Scott, 1971.

Marsh, J. "The Book of Numbers." In *The Interpreter's Bible,* vol. II, pp. 137-308. Ed. G. A. Buttrick, et. al. New York: Abingdon Press, 1953.

Mays, J. L. *The Book of Leviticus. The Book of Numbers.* The Layman's Bible Commentary. Richmond, Virgina: John Knox Press, 1963.

_____. *Micah: A Commentary.* The Old Testament Library. Philadelphia: Westminster Press, 1976.

Moran, W. L. "Deuteronomy." In *A New Catholic Commentary on Holy Scripture,* pp. 256-76. Ed. R. C. Fuller, L. Johnston and C. Kearns. Camden, New Jersey: Thomas Nelson and Sons, 1969.

Myers, J. M. *I Chronicles.* The Anchor Bible. Garden City, New York: Doubleday and Co., 1965.

Noth, M. *Exodus: A Commentary.* Trans. J. S. Bowden. The Old Testament Library. Philadelphia: Westminster Press, 1962.

_____. *Numbers: A Commentary.* Trans. J. D. Martin. The Old Testament Library. Philadelphia: Westminster Press, 1968.

Phillips, A. *Deuteronomy.* The Cambridge Bible Commentary. Cambridge: Cambridge University Press, 1973.

Rad, G. von. *Deuteronomy: A Commentary.* Trans. D. Barton. The Old Testament Liberary. Philadelphia: Westminster Press, 1966.

Ryan, D. "Micah." In *A New Catholic Commentary on Holy Scripture,* pp. 708-12. Ed. R. C. Fuller, L. Johnston, C. Kearns. New York: Thomas Nelson and Sons, 1969.

Rylaarsdam, J. C. "The Book of Exodus." In *The Interpreter's Bible,* vol. I, pp. 833-1099. Ed. G. A. Buttrick, et. al. New York: Abingdon Press, 1952.

Scott, R. B. Y. "The Book of Isaiah." In *The Interpreter's Bible,* vol. V, pp. 151-773. Ed. G. A. Buttrick, et. al. New York: Abingdon Press, 1956.

Slotki, I. W., *Isaiah.* Soncino Books of the Bible. London: Soncino Press, 1949.

Smith, J. M. P.; Ward, W. H. and Bewer, J. A. *A Critical and Exegetical Commentary on Micah, Zephaniah, Nahum, Habakkuk, Obadiah and Joel.* The International Critical Commentary. New York: Charles Scribner's Sons, 1911.

Snaith, N. H. "The First and Second Books of Kings." In *The Interpreter's Bible,* vol. III, pp. 3-338. Ed. G. A. Buttrick, et. al. New York: Abingdon Press, 1954.

_____. *Leviticus and Numbers.* The Century Bible. Camden, New Jersey: Thomas Nelson and Sons, 1967.

Thomas, D. W. "Micah." In *Peake's Commentary on the Bible*, pp. 630-34.
Ed. M. Black and H. H. Rowley. New York: Thomas Nelson and Sons,
1963.

Thompson, J. A. *Deuteronomy: An Introduction and a Commentary*. Tyndale Old Testament Commentaries. London: Inter-Varsity Press,
1974.

Weiser, A. *The Psalms*. Trans. H. Hartwell. The Old Testament Library.
Philadelphia: Westminster Press, 1962.

Wolfe, R. E. "The Book of Micah." In *The Interpreter's Bible*, vol. VI, pp.
897-949. Ed. G. A. Buttrick, et. al. New York: Abingdon Press, 1956.

Wright, G. E. "The Book of Deuteronomy." In *The Interpreter's Bible*, vol.
II, pp. 311-537. Ed. G. A. Buttrick, et. al. New York: Abingdon Press,
1953.

Young, E. J. *The Book of Isaiah*, vol. 1. The New International Commentary on the Old Testament. Grand Rapids, Michigan: William B.
Eerdmans, 1965.

OTHER WORKS CITED

Albright, W. F. "A Catalogue of Early Hebrew Lyric Poems (Psalm
LXVIII)." *Hebrew Union College Annual* 23 (1950), 1-39.

_____. *Yahweh and the Gods of Canaan*. London: Athlone Press,
1968.

Anderson, B. W. and Harrelson, W., eds. *Israel's Prophetic Heritage:
Essays in Honor of James Muilenberg*. New York: Harper and Row,
1962.

Andriolo, K. R. "A Structural Analysis of Genealogy and Worldview in the
Old Testament." *American Anthropologist* 75 (1973), 1657-69.

Backman, E. L. *Religious Dances*. Trans. E. Classen. London: George Allen
and Unwin, 1952.

Bauer, H. "Die Gottheiten von Ras Shamra." *Zeitschrift für die alttestamentliche Wissenschaft* 51 (1933), 81-101.

_____. "Die Gottheiten von Ras Shamra." *Zeitschrift für die alttes-
tamentliche Wissenschaft* 53 (1935), 54-59.

Bentzen, A. "The Cultic Use of the Story of the Ark in Samuel." *Journal
of Biblical Literature* 67 (1948), 37-53.

Beyerlin, W. *Origins and History of the Oldest Sinaitic Traditions*. Trans.
S. Rudman. Oxford: Basil Blackwell, 1965.

Bird, P. "Images of Women in the Old Testament." In *Religion and Sexism: Images of Women in the Jewish and Christian Traditions*, pp. 41-88. Ed. Rosemary R. Ruether. New York: Simon and Schuster, 1974.

Blackman, A. "On the Position of Women in the Ancient Egyptian Hierarchy." *Journal of Egyptian Archaeology* 7 (1921), 8-30.

Blenkinsopp, J. "Ballad Style and Psalm Style in the Song of Deborah: A Discussion." *Biblica* 42 (1961), 61-76.

_____ "Kiriath-jearim and the Ark." *Journal of Biblical Literature* 88 (1969), 143-56.

Breyfogle, C. "The Religious Status of Woman in the Old Testament." *Biblical World* 35 (1910), 405-19.

Carroll, R. P. "The Elijah-Elisha Sagas: Some Remarks on Prophetic Succession in Ancient Israel." *Vetus Testamentum* 19 (1969), 400-15.

_____ "Rebellion and Dissent in Ancient Israelite Society." *Zeitschrift für die alttestamentliche Wissenschaft* 89 (1977), 176-204.

Coats, G. W. *Rebellion in the Wilderness: The Murmuring Motif in the Wilderness Traditions of the Old Testament*. Nashville: Abingdon Press, 1968.

_____. "The Wilderness Itinerary." *Catholic Biblical Quarterly* 34 (1972), 135-52.

Cody, A. *A History of Old Testament Priesthood*. Analecta Biblica 35. Rome: Pontifical Biblical Institute, 1969.

Craigie, P. C. "The Song of Deborah and the Epic of Tukulti-Ninurta." *Journal of Biblical Literature* 88 (1969), 253-65.

Crenshaw, J. L. *Prophetic Conflict: Its Effect Upon Israelite Religion*. Berlin: Walter de Gruyter, 1971.

Cross, F. M., Jr. *Canaanite Myth and Hebrew Epic*. Cambridge: Harvard University Press, 1973.

_____ "The Divine Warrior in Israel's Early Cult." In *Biblical Motifs: Origins and Transformations*, pp. 11-30. Ed. A. Altmann. Cambridge: Harvard University Press, 1966.

_____ and Freedman, D. N. "The Song of Miriam." *Journal of Near Eastern Studies* 14 (1955), 237-50.

Culley, R. C. *Studies in the Structures of Hebrew Narrative*. Missoula, Montana: Scholars Press, 1976.

De Vries, S. J. "The Origin of the Murmuring Tradition." *Journal of Biblical Literature* 87 (1968), 51-58.

Driver, G. R. and Miles, J. C. *The Babylonian Laws.* 2 vols. Oxford: Clarendon Press, 1955 (vol. I); 1952, 1960 (vol. II).

Eissfeldt, O. *The Old Testament: An Introduction.* Trans. P. Ackroyd. New York: Harper and Row, 1965.

Engnell, I. *Studies in Divine Kingship in the Ancient Near East.* Oxford: Basil Blackwell, 1967.

Erman, A. *Die Ägyptische Religion.* 2nd ed. Berlin, 1901.

Fensham, F. C. "The Battle Between the Men of Joab and Abner as a Possible Ordeal by Battle?" *Vetus Testamentum* 20 (1970), 356-57.

Freedman, D. N. "The Aaronic Benediction (Numbers 6:24-26." In *No Famine in the Land: Studies in Honor of John L. McKenzie,* pp. 35-48. Ed. J. M. Flanagan and A. W. Robinson. Missoula, Montana: Scholars Press, 1975.

_____. "Isaiah 42,13." *Catholic Biblical Quarterly* 30 (1968), 225-26.

_____. "The Chronicler's Purpose." *Catholic Biblical Quarterly* 23 (1961), 436-42.

Fritz, V. *Israel in der Wüste.* Marburg: N. G. Elwert, 1970.

Gardiner, A. H. "The Egyptian Origin of Some English Personal Names." *Journal of the American Oriental Society* 56 (1936), 189-97.

Gemser, B. "The Rîb-Pattern in Hebrew Mentality." In *Wisdom in Israel and in the Ancient Near East,* pp. 120-37. Ed. M. Noth and D. Winton Thomas. Leiden: Brill, 1955.

Gervitz, S. *Patterns in Early Hebrew Poetry.* Chicago: University of Chicago Press, 1963.

Gottwald, N. K. "Immanuel as the Prophet's Son." *Vetus Testamentum* 8 (1958), 36-47.

Gray, G. B. *Sacrifice in the Old Testament: Its Theory and Practice.* 1925; reprint ed. The Library of Biblical Studies. New York: Ktav Publishing House, 1971.

Gray, J. *Near Eastern Mythology.* London: Hamlyn Publishing Group, 1969.

Gunkel, H. *The Psalms: A Form-Critical Introduction.* Trans. T. M. Horner. Philadelphia: Fortress Press (Facet Books), 1967.

Haldar, A. *Associations of Cult Prophets Among the Ancient Semites.* Uppsala, 1945.

Hamlin, E. J. "The Commissioning Ordeal of the Liberator: A Study of Exodus 4:1-9." *Southeast Asia Journal of Theology* 11 (1969), 64-71.

Hanson, P. D. "The Song of Heshbon and David's Nîr." *Harvard Theological Review* 61 (1968) 297-320.

Haran, M. "From Early to Classical Prophecy: Continuity and Change." *Vetus Testamentum* 27 (1977), 385-97.

Herbert, A. S. *Worship in Ancient Israel.* Ecumenical Studies in Worship 5. London: Butterworth Press, 1959.

Heschel, A. J. *The Prophets.* New York: Harper and Row, 1963.

Hillers, D. R. "Ritual Procession of the Ark and Ps. 132." *Catholic Biblical Quarterly* 30 (1968), 48-55.

Hösl, I. "Zur orientalischen Namenkunde: Maria-Moses-Aaron: Eine philologische Studie." In *Serta Monacensia: Franz Babinger zum 15. Januar 1951 als Festgruss Dargebracht,* pp. 80-83. Ed. H. J. Kissling and A. Schmaus. Leiden: Brill, 1952.

Hoffner, H. A., Jr. "A Hittite Analogue to the David and Goliath Contest of Champions?" *Catholic Biblical Quarterly* 30 (1968), 220-25.

Holladay, W. L. "The Background of Jeremiah's Self-Understanding: Moses, Samuel and Psalm 22." *Journal of Biblical Literature* 83 (1964), 153-64.

_____ "Jeremiah and Moses: Further Observations." *Journal of Biblical Literature* 85 (1966), 17-27.

Huffmon, H. B. "The Covenant Lawsuit in the Prophets." *Journal of Biblical Literature* 78 (1959), 285-95.

Humbert, P. "Der Name Meri-baʿal." *Zeitschrift für die alttestamentliche Wissenschaft* 38 (1919-20), 86.

Hvidberg, F. F. *Weeping and Laughter in the Old Testament.* Copenhagen, 1962.

Jeppesen, K. "New Aspects of Micah Research." *Journal for the Study of the Old Testament* 8 (1978), 3-32.

Johnson, A. R. *The Cultic Prophet in Ancient Israel.* 2nd ed. Cardiff: University of Wales Press, 1962.

_____. "Hebrew Conceptions of Kingship." In *Myth, Ritual and Kingship: Essays on the Theory and Practice of Kingship in the Ancient Near East and in Israel*, pp. 204-35. Ed. S. H. Hooke. Oxford: Clarendon Press, 1958.

Johnson, M. D. *The Purpose of Biblical Genealogies*. Society for New Testament Studies 8. Cambridge: Cambridge University Press, 1969.

Kraus, H. J. *Worship in Israel*. Trans. G. Buswell. Richmond, Virginia: John Knox Press, 1966.

Kselman, J. S. "A Note on Nm. XII 6-8." *Vetus Testamentum* 26 (1976), 500-505.

Kuhl, C. *The Prophets of Israel*. Trans. R. J. Ehrlich and J. P. Smith. Richmond, Virginia: John Knox Press, 1960.

Laughlin, J. C. H. "The 'Strange Fire' of Nadab and Abihu." *Journal of Biblical Literature* 75 (1976), 559-65.

Le Déaut, R. "Miryam, soeur de Moïse, et Marie, mère du Messie." *Biblica* 45 (1964), 198-219.

Leeuw, G. van der. *Religion in Essence and Manifestation*. Trans. J. E. Turner. London: George Allen and Unwin. 1938.

Limburg, J. "The Root ריב and the Prophetic Lawsuit Speeches." *Journal of Biblical Literature* 88 (1969), 291-304.

Lindblom, J. *Prophecy in Ancient Israel*. Philadelphia: Muhlenberg Press, 1962.

May, H. G. "An Interpretation of the Names of Hosea's Children." *Journal of Biblical Literature* 55 (1936), 285-91.

Mayes, A. D. H. "The Rise of the Israelite Monarachy." *Zeitschrift für die alttestamentlich Wissenschaft* 90 (1978), 1-19.

Mendenhall, G. E. "The Census Lists of Numbers 1 and 26." *Journal of Biblical Literature* 77 (1958), 52-66.

_____ "Covenant Forms in Israelite Tradition." In *The Biblical Archaeologist Reader*, vol. 3, pp. 25-53. Ed. E. F. Campbell, Jr. and D. N. Freedman. Garden City, New York: Doubleday (Anchor Books), 1970.

Miller, P. D., Jr. *The Divine Warrior in Early Israel*. Cambridge: Harvard University Press, 1973.

Mowinckel, S. *Der Achtundsechzigste Psalm*. Oslo: I Kommisjon hos Jacob Dybwad, 1953.

_____. "Drive and/or Ride in O. T." *Vetus Testamentum* 12 (1962), 278-99.

_____. *He That Cometh.* Trans. G. W. Anderson. Oxford: Basil Blackwell, 1956.

_____. *The Psalms in Israel's Worship.* 2 vols. Trans. D. R. Ap-Thomas. Oxford: Basil Blackewell, 1962.

Muilenberg, J. "A Liturgy on the Triumphs of Yahweh." In *Studia Biblica et Semitica,* Vriezen Volume, pp. 233-51. Wageningen: H. Veenman & Zonen N.V., 1966.

_____. "The 'Office' of the Prophet in Ancient Israel." In *The Bible in Modern Scholarship,* pp. 74-97. Ed. J. Philip Hyatt. Nashville: Abingdon, 1965.

Nicholson, E. W. "The Antiquity of the Tradition in Ex. XXIV 9-11." *Vetus Testamentum* 25 (1975), 69-79.

_____. *Deuteronomy and Tradition.* Philadelphia: Fortress Press, 1967.

_____. "The Interpretation of Ex. XXIV 9-11." *Vetus Testamentum* 24 (1974), pp. 77-97.

_____. "The Tradition in Ex. XXIV 9-11." *Vetus Testamentum* 26 (1976), 148-60.

North, R. J. "Theology of the Chronicler." *Journal of Biblical Literature* 82 (1963), 369-81.

Noth, M. *A History of Pentateuchal Traditions.* Trans. B. W. Anderson. Englewood Cliffs, New Jersey: Prentice-Hall, 1972.

_____. *Die israelitischen Personennamen im Rahmen der gemeinsemitischen Namengebung.* Hildesheim: Georg Olms, 1966.

_____. *The Laws in the Pentateuch and Other Studies.* Trans. D. R. Ap-Thomas. Philadelphia: Fortress Press, 1966.

_____. "The 'Re-presentation' of the O.T. in Proclamation." In *Essays on Old Testament Hermeneutics,* pp. 76-88. Ed. C. Westermann. English trans. ed. J. L. Mays. Richmond, Virginia: John Knox Press, 1963.

Oesterley, W. O. E. *The Sacred Dance.* New York: MacMillan, 1923.

Otwell, J. H. *And Sarah Laughed: The Status of Women in the Old Testament.* Philadelphia: Westminster Press, 1977.

Pedersen, J. *Israel: Its Life and Culture*. Vols. 3-4. London: Oxford University Press, 1940.

Peritz, I. "Women in Ancient Hebrew Cult." *Journal of Biblical Literature* 17 (1898), 111-48.

Pfeiffer, R. H. *Introduction to the Old Testament*. New York: Harper and Brothers, 1948.

Porter, J. R. "The Interpretation of 2 Samuel VI and Psalm CXXXII." *Journal of Theological Studies* 5 (1954), 161-73.

Pritchard, J. B., ed. *Ancient Near Eastern Texts Relating to the Old Testament*. 2nd ed. Princeton, New Jersey: Princeton University Press, 1955.

Rad, G. von. *Old Testament Theology*. Trans. D. M. G. Stalker. 2 vols. New York: Harper and Row, 1962 (vol. 1); 1965 (vol. 2).

_____ *The Problem of the Hexateuch and Other Essays*. Trans. E. W. Trueman Dicken. New York: McGraw-Hill, 1966.

_____ *Studies in Deuteronomy*. Trans. D. Stalker. Chicago: Henry Regnery, 1953.

Ringgren, W. *Religions of the Ancient Near East*. Trans. J. Sturdy. Philadelphia: Westminster Press, 1973.

Robinson, R. B. "The Levites in the Pre-Monarchical Period." *Studia Biblica et Theologica* 8 (1978), 3-24.

Ross, J. F. "Miriam." In *The Interpreter's Dictionary of the Bible*, vol. 3, p. 402. Ed. G. A. Buttrick, et al. New York: Abingdon Press, 1962.

Roth, W. M. W. "The Numerical Sequence x/x+1 in the Old Testament." *Vetus Testamentum* 12 (1962), 300-311.

Rozelaar, M. "The Song of the Sea (Exodus XV, 1b-18)." *Vetus Testamentum* 2 (1952), 221-28.

Saggs, H. W. F. *The Greatness That Was Babylon*. London: Sidgewick and Jackson, 1962.

Sasson, J. M. "Numbers 5 and the 'Waters of Judgment'." *Biblische Zeitschrift* 16 (1972), 249-51.

Sauneron, S. *The Priests of Ancient Egypt*. Trans. A. Morrissett. New York: Grove Press, 1960.

Schmidt, H. "Das Meerlied: Ex. 15, 2-19." *Zeitschrift für die alttestamentliche Wissenschaft* 49 (1931), 59-66.

Sheehan, J. F. X. "The Pre-P Narrative: A Children's Recital?" In *Scripture in History and Theology: Essays in Honor of J. Coert Rylaarsdam*, pp. 25-46. Ed. A. L. Merrill and T. W. Overholt. Pittsburgh: Pickwick Press, 1977.

Simpson, C. A. *The Early Traditions of Israel: A Critical Analysis of the Pre-deuteronomic Narrative of the Hexateuch*. Oxford: Basil Blackwell, 1948.

Smith, W. *Kinship and Marriage in Early Arabia*. London: A. and C. Black, 1903; reprint ed. Boston: Beacon Press, n.d.

_____. *Lectures on the Religion of the Semites: The Fundamental Institutions*. 1927; reprint 3rd ed., New York: Ktav Publishing House, 1969.

Tillesse, G. Minette de. "Sections 'tu' et sections 'vous' dans le Deuteronome." *Vetus Testamentum* 12 (1962), 29-87.

Tucker, G. M. "Prophetic Speech." *Interpretation* 32 (1978), 31-45.

Tunyogi, A. "The Rebellions of Israel." *Journal of Biblical Literature* 81 (1962), 385-90.

_____. *The Rebellions of Israel*. Richmond, Virginia: John Knox Press, 1969.

Vaux, R. de. *Ancient Israel*. Vol. 2: *Religious Institutions*. New York: McGraw-Hill Paperbacks, 1965; part IV of original ed., *Ancient Israel: Its Life and Institutions*, trans. J. McHugh. New York: McGraw-Hill, 1961.

_____. *The Early History of Israel*. Trans. D. Smith. Philadelphia: Westminster Press, 1978.

Vos, C. J. *Woman in Old Testament Worship*. Delft: Judels & Brinkman, 1968.

Walsh, J. T. "From Egypt to Moab: A Source Critical Analysis of the Wilderness Itinerary." *Catholic Biblical Quarterly* 39 (1977), 20-33.

Watson, P. "Form Criticism and an Exegesis of Micah 6: 1-8." *Restoration Quarterly* 7 (1963), 61-72.

Weiser, A. *The Old Testament: Its Formation and Development*. Trans. D. M. Barton. New York: Association Press, 1961.

Westermann, C. *Basic Forms of Prophetic Speech*. Trans. H. C. White. Philadelphia: Westminster Press, 1967.

_____. *The Praise of God in the Psalms*. Trans. K. R. Crim. Richmond, Virginia: John Knox Press, 1965.

Wilcoxen, J. A. "Some Anthropocentric Aspects of Israel's Sacred History." *Journal of Religion* 48 (1968), 333-50.

Willis, J. T. "The Structure of the Book of Micah." *Svensk Exegetisk Årsbok* 34 (1969), 5-42.

_____. "The Structure, Setting and Interrelationships of the Pericopes in the Book of Micah." Ph.D. dissertation, Vanderbilt Divinity School, 1966.

Wilson, R. R. "Early Israelite Prophecy." *Interpretation* 32 (1978), 3-16.

_____. *Genealogy and History in the Biblical World*. Yale Near Eastern Researches, 7. New Haven: Yale University Press, 1977.

_____. "The Old Testament Genealogies in Recent Research," *Journal of Biblical Literature* 94 (1975), 169-89.

Wolf, H. M. "A Solution to the Imanuel Prophecy in Isaiah 7:14-8:22." *Journal of Biblical Literature* 91 (1972), 449-56.

Zorell, F. "Was bedeutet der Name Maria?" *Zeitschrift für katholische Theologie* 30 (1906), 356-60.